W9-AVI-274

THE DEITY FORMERLY KNOWN AS

GOD

THE DEITY FORMERLY KNOWN AS

GOD

JARRETT STEVENS

ZONDERVAN®

GRAND RAPIDS, MICHIGAN 49530 USA

WILLOW

Willow Creek Resources

ZONDERVAN.COM/
AUTHORTRACKER

ZONDERVAN®

The Deity Formerly Known as God
Copyright © 2006 by Jarrett Stevens

Requests for information should be addressed to:
Zondervan, *Grand Rapids, Michigan 49530*

Library of Congress Cataloging-in-Publication Data

Stevens, Jarrett.
    The deity formerly known as God / Jarrett Stevens.—1st ed.
      p. cm.
    Includes bibliographical references.
    ISBN-10: 0-310-27114-2
    ISBN-13: 978-0-310-27114-7
    1. God. I. Title.
  BT103.S74 2006
  231—dc22

                                     2006009336

All Scripture quotations, unless otherwise indicated, are taken from the *Holy Bible: Today's New International Version™*. TNIV®. Copyright © 2001, 2005 by International Bible Society. Used by permission of Zondervan. All rights reserved.

Scripture quotations marked NLT are taken from the *Holy Bible: New Living Translation*, copyright © 1996. Used by permission of Tyndale House Publishers, Inc., Wheaton, Illinois. All rights reserved.

Scripture quotations marked MSG are taken from *The Message*. Copyright © 1993, 1994, 1995, 1996, 2000, 2001, 2002. Used by permission of NavPress Publishing Group.

The website addresses recommended throughout this book are offered as a resource to you. These websites are not intended in any way to be or imply an endorsement on the part of Zondervan, nor do we vouch for their content for the life of this book.

All rights reserved. No part of this publication may be reproduced, stored in a retrieval system, or transmitted in any form or by any means—electronic, mechanical, photocopy, recording, or any other—except for brief quotations in printed reviews, without the prior permission of the publisher.

Interior illustration by Curtis Anderson

ABBA photo: Michael Ochs Archives/Corbis Images

Interior design by Michelle Espinoza

Printed in the United States of America

06 07 08 09 10 11 12 • 15 14 13 12 11 10 9 8 7 6 5 4 3 2 1

*I dedicate this book to my wife Jeannie.
You are my lover, friend, truth-speaker, partner.
Your relentless commitment to helping all
of who I am love and trust God for all he is,
has been not only the inspiration and
motivation for this book, but for my life.*

*And to Elijah William Stevens,
our beautiful baby boy who was born
in the midst of the writing of this book.
You are our greatest endeavor and our greatest joy.
We love you, desire you, and delight in you.*

Contents

Acknowledgments

There are a few people I would like to thank. First off, this book would not be in your hands if it weren't for my spiritual director and friend Sheryl Fleisher. Sheryl gave two years' worth of Tuesday mornings to making sure I was doing the work of unpacking my own destructive images of God. If these words carry any soul-connecting truth, they can be directly traced back to the way God has used Sheryl in my life.

I would also like to thank my church, Willow Creek, and specifically the Axis Community. For the last seven years you have been my own spiritual community. You have inspired me to dive deeper into my own understanding and experience with God. Most of the stories in this book you've heard before; please find it in your heart to laugh at them one more time.

Also, I would like to thank Christine Anderson at the Willow Creek Association and Angela Scheff at Zondervan. You both have done so much to make this book a reality. Thank you for all your help and work in drawing out the essence of this book from the ADD wonderland I call my brain.

Thanks to John Raymond at Zondervan. You have been such a wonderful advocate for me and for this book.

To my friend Curtis Anderson, who did the visual design for this book. Your work is exactly what I knew I wanted before a word was even written. I love working with you.

To my family (both the Pieczynskis and the Stevenses). You are my greatest source of love and my greatest source of material.

To my friends who have walked with me through life and through the process of this book. Thank you for all your help in keeping me and this book true to who I am.

To Cliff and Judy Fenton, thank you for your incredible generosity in allowing us to stay at your home in Colorado. It was there that the bulk of this book was written.

And to anyone who would actually take the time to read this entire thank-you list. You really are committed to getting your money's worth out of this book.

Before You Begin

God created people in his image on the sixth day, and every day since, people have returned the favor.

Blaise Pascal

*T*wasn't really sure where it came from. I didn't remember buying it or borrowing it, but there it was on my bookshelf—small, slightly faded, and patiently waiting to be discovered. I didn't think much of it at the time; it wasn't like the face of Jesus had suddenly appeared in my Special K. I was just looking for a good book on sex for a sermon I was working on. But there it was, this little blue book by J. B. Phillips titled *Your God Is Too Small*.

After a little bit of "googling," I discovered that Phillips, a prolific British Bible translator, wrote the book in 1952 in response to his generation's unquenchable desire to elevate humankind, specifically the capacity of the rational human mind, to near-godlike status. It was a time in this little planet's history when reason eclipsed faith and God was confined to the cage of proof and principle. So in response to the spiritual conversation of his day, Phillips wrote *Your God Is Too Small*.

He devoted the first half of his book to deconstructing—with brutal honesty—many of the destructive images of God that kept people from seeing God for who he really is. In the second half of the book, Phillips reconstructed a logical framework for understanding the truth of who God is. With the precision of a seasoned surgeon and the heart of a pastor, Phillips spoke spiritual truth into a generation that was steeped in the slowly crumbling ideals of the Modern Era.

Over fifty years later, this little blue book still speaks to our society, but much has changed. Modernism is in the final stages of rigor mortis, while postmodernism tentatively takes its place on the throne of culture. While our questions and preconceived notions of God may differ from those of Phillips's generation (as you'll see throughout the first part of this book), we share the same basic problem: our insistence on crafting images of God that limit our understanding of ourselves and limit our experience with God. We'd rather have a small, custom-built God who meets our emotional needs or suits our intellectual ideals, than a big God who can't be controlled or contained.

While Phillips's book didn't help me much with my sermon preparation, it did help me unearth some personal misconceptions of God that had taken root in the soil of my soul. *Your God Is Too Small* stirred up questions in me that I had to muster up the courage to ask. Have I crafted my own version of God? Where did it come from? Have some of my friends done the same?

To my surprise, I was not the only one on this journey of unpacking and understanding the truth about God. Shortly after working through Phillips's book, I began to notice how it was taking on a life of its own in my friends' lives. I saw this when I began to work out some of these thoughts in a series of sermons I called "The Deity Formerly Known as God." As I shared the content of Phillips's work with the Axis community at Willow Creek (where I am a pastor), I saw that it was often as eye-opening for them as it was for me. But I began to notice that, while this book still had a voice, much of its language and many of the images of God Phillips used could stand an upgrade, a remix if you will. Enter the book you now hold in your hands.

This Is the Remix

The Deity Formerly Known as God is an attempt to recapture the spirit and power of J. B. Phillips's original work for the days we find ourselves in. In keeping with Phillips's two-part structure, the first half of this book uncovers a few of the destructive images of God we've created, while the second half of the book explores some constructive images Jesus used to describe God. Perhaps the greatest difference between Phillips's work and this project is that the constructive images here draw heavily on the vivid, unexpected, and downright shocking manner in which Jesus described God. The images Jesus used are so much better than any of my flannelgraph flashbacks. His words are alive, challenging, common, and yet somehow beyond anything we'd ever expect. After all, you've got to figure that if anyone knew God or knew how to talk about him, it had to be Jesus.

Throughout this book, you'll find that I tell a lot of stories. I love stories. Some of the stories are from the Bible, some are from my life. These are the stories that I know. They serve as small illuminators of great truth to me. I don't propose for a second to know all of the answers to the questions that have arisen on this journey or that might arise from this book, only the stories that have led me to this point and the stories that lead me back to God.

My hope is that by exploring and wrestling with the images of God found in this book, you will begin to work through your own broken and destructive images and arrive at a healthy, life-giving, mind-blowing, heart-expanding experience with God. That's the destination. How you get there though is entirely up to you. This book works less like a recipe and more like a menu. So feel free to chart your own path for how you travel through these pages. This introduction (which you are conveniently reading) is the only chapter you need to read before reading any of the following chapters in their respective sections. If it helps to read chapter by chapter, go for it. If you want to skip ahead and just read part 2, be my guest. Maybe you'll want to reflect on it privately, or maybe you'll want to talk about it with some friends over a cup of coffee, or both. It's really up to you. I'm not here to tell you how to read it. My hope is that in some way, this book will help you begin to realize that God is and always has been so much greater, more powerful, and more amazing than our little minds can comprehend and than a little book like this can contain. And I hope you'll see that the ancient promise of Jeremiah 29:13 still holds true today: that if you will seek out the real God, not only will you find him, but in so doing, you will find the real you as well.

Part 1

Destructive Images We've Shaped

Cop around the Corner

Not long ago, I took a short road trip with my wife Jeanne and her mom Peggy. About two hours into our trip, I was shocked to discover that in her thirty-plus years of driving, my mother-in-law had never been pulled over for speeding. Not even once. In fact, she had driven thirty-five years without a single ticket on her record! I don't even know how to comprehend that reality. In the first year I had my license, I successfully managed to drive over a curb and drop eight feet into a creek, sideswipe a parked car, and receive the first in a long line of speeding tickets. On that road trip I came to two conclusions: (1) my mother-in-law has no clue about the fear that plagues most drivers when they see a parked cop car, and (2) she should probably be the one to drive for the rest of our trip.

As hard as it is to believe, I know she is not the only one of her kind. There are others like her. In fact, you may be someone who knows nothing of the fear and anxiety people go through every time they see a black-and-white sedan on the side of the road. On the slim chance this describes you, then please read on with a sense of empathy and understanding for the rest of us ... and feel free at any time to wipe that smug smile off your face.

Unless there is a God by whom "right" and "wrong" can be reliably assessed, moral judgements can be no more than opinion, influenced by upbringing, training, and propaganda.

J. B. Phillips

Every time I see a parked police car hiding around the corner with its lights off and the silhouette of someone pointing what appears to be a hair dryer in my general direction, I instinctively freeze. I convince myself that if I'm really, really still, the officer won't notice as I fly past at thirty-seven miles per hour over the speed limit. Without even thinking, I run through a series of routine quick checks. I check my seatbelt, using only my hands, like a pat down at an airport security check. I check to see if anyone else around me might be doing something more illegal than me. I make sure to turn down the radio, not knowing what difference that makes but feeling like it's a good idea. I rack my brain to remember if there's anything in my Pandora's box of a glove compartment that remotely resembles an insurance or registration card. All the while checking my rearview mirror every 1.7 seconds, stomach clenched, wondering if I'll see the flashing reds and blues.

Getting caught by a police officer can make a person do crazy things. Everyone reacts in different ways, the only similarity being that no one seems to remain themselves. Something changes. Getting pulled over makes otherwise calm and collected people go absolutely nuts, and we have the footage to prove it. Watch just a few minutes of any "dash-cam" cop show and you'll see soccer moms transform into purse-swinging gladiators. And tranquil trigonometry teachers become cursing sailors. For some, the excuses fly like clothes off the rack at a going-out-of-business sale. For others, tears flow like broken fire hydrants in a Brooklyn summer. I have another response. I become the nicest, most clueless guy a cop has ever met. I act completely surprised. I insert the words "sir" or "ma'am" as much as possible. I reassure the officer that I am just as surprised as they are, all the while shaking my head at my speedometer, shocked at how it could betray our longstanding unspoken agreement.

Everyone reacts to the fear of getting caught by a cop in one way or another. It's moments like these that reveal some of my deepest fears and anxieties. My fear of being caught, my willingness and readiness to lie or make excuses, my panicked impulse to floor it and pull a Thelma and Louise. That fear is always somewhere within me, every time I get in the car, everywhere I go. And all it takes to bring it to the surface is a cop around the corner.

✦ ══════ ✦

I often wonder if it's really just a cop we're most afraid of, or if it's actually something much deeper. If all it takes are a couple of flashing lights and a squealing siren to evoke such deep emotions and reactions, then imagine what the soul goes through when it fears it's been found out by God. What fears and anxieties rise to the surface at the slightest thought of being "caught" by God?

My hunch is that many of us move through this life operating under the same basic set of cosmic assumptions:

- There actually is a permanent record out there filled with all the wrong things I've ever done.

- I'm probably doing something wrong right now.

- At this very moment, God is lurking around some dark corner of my life with his radar gun, just waiting to nail me for whatever it is so he can add yet another entry to my permanent record.

Sadly for some, this is all they have to point to as their "faith experience." An experience that operates in a fear-based system. This assumption about God tends to take root early in life and is connected to some negative experience with an authority figure — a parent, teacher, coach, boss, or just about anyone else who had power over us. My friend Ryan can pinpoint the precise moment this fear was formed in him.

When he was in fifth grade his family lived abroad, and he was forced to attend a religious boarding school with a strict dress and grooming code (apparently there's a verse in the Old Testament that says the Devil is in the denim). When he returned to school after a summer break, the headmaster noticed that Ryan's hair hung in rebellion about two inches over the tops of his ears. And Ryan wasn't the only one. Infuriated at such disregard for the rules, the headmaster immediately and forcibly marched all the little members of that mullet militia onto a beat-up school bus. They drove in silence for almost an hour, having no idea where they were going. When the bus pulled up in front of the local Air Force base, the boys were escorted across the massive facility into the base barber shop. Air Force barbers proceeded to shave the boys' heads in record military time. As hair and tears gathered on the linoleum floor, the headmaster laid down the law. "God is a God of rules, boys," he barked. "God gives us rules and those who enforce the rules to keep us from getting out of control. Let this be a lesson to you, boys."

The headmaster had no idea how effective his lesson was. It would take another eight years from that moment until Ryan could even begin to consider the concept of a loving God. And another eight years from that moment until he began to seek out this God. And of course, it would be many more years still until Ryan even considered wearing his hair short again.

Can you pinpoint an experience or person who first planted a toxic fear of God in you? It may have been a rule-ridden principal, rule-ridden parents, or some sort of rule-ridden religion. Sadly, without even knowing it, it is possible that you've become a rule-ridden person yourself—someone whose whole life is built around playing by the rules. Someone who avoids more than enjoys and is more familiar with fear than freedom. Someone who loves the idea of a citizen's arrest and makes as many of them as possible. You can find them almost anywhere, pointing fingers, whispering judgment, and running to tattle to a God who loves to catch people screwing up. They embody what Anne Lamott was getting at when she wrote, "You can tell you have created God in your own image when it turns out that he or she hates all the same people you do."[1] Sadly, if you grew up around church or religion, it doesn't take long for images of these folks to come to mind. You may know more of these folks than you would like to admit. You may even have become one yourself.

Rule-ridden people abound because we live in a culture that depends on behavior management. It's a culture that is quick to punish bad behavior and wrong choices, but does very little to reward good choices or good behavior. I have yet to receive a letter from the IRS thanking me

1. Anne Lamott, *Bird by Bird* (New York: Random House, 1994).

for turning in my taxes on time. In all my years of driving I've never been pulled over by a cop who just wanted to express appreciation for how I used my blinker in that last lane change, or to commend my firm grasp of the "right-of-way" concept. It doesn't happen. It probably never will. But turn in my taxes a few weeks late or cross a double yellow line, and someone is right there to bust me. I'm motivated to do my taxes on time and stick to my side of the road, not because these things are right or good, but simply because I don't want to be caught and punished.

So if you believe in a God who created the world we live in, then you have to wonder if God operates according to the same system. Is this whole fear-based system something that God actually created to keep us all in line? Connect the dots. If the primary role of authority in our world is to enforce all the rules and punish those who don't follow them, and if God is the "ultimate authority," doesn't it make sense that God's primary role in this world and in your life consists of enforcing the rules and punishing those who break them? Sure, God makes the sun rise and set, paints the occasional rainbow, and sure, God makes puppies with their cute little faces and fur so soft you can't help but kiss it, but corner God, and he'll tell you, the thing he is most interested in is whether or not you keep all the rules.

For hundreds and hundreds of years, "keeping the rules" has been the primary focus of what we have come to call religion. Accumulated "goodness," and/or lack of "badness," defines the depth of our devotion to God. Goodness and badness are what matter most in this kind of "religion," so they must be what matter most to God.

Reflect for a moment on God's track record. Perhaps you've read God's résumé or heard stories about how, on more than one occasion, the Lord Almighty didst smite large numbers of evil (rule-breaking) people. In the Old Testament there are more than a few stories of God destroying entire nations who were guilty of breaking the rules (and it's not always clear that they even knew there were rules to begin with!). These stories are more than complicated; they can be downright disturbing. They lead more to complex questions than to simple answers. What really matters most to God? Is not doing wrong more important than doing right? If not, then why are there so many rules?

Thumb through the first couple books of the Old Testament and it seems as though every other page features a new set of rules to follow, each set raising the bar to an impossible level of perfection that God somehow expects us to live up to.

If God is nothing more than a rule keeper or a commandment maker, then why would anyone want anything to do with him? If that's all there is to it, then there is nothing intimate or personal about him ... or about us, for that matter. In fact, if that's all there is to it, then we're nothing but a few more faces in a long lineup of perpetrators who need to be caught and corrected.

Is this the only God you've ever known? A God who demands respect over admiration? Who would rather speak through lectures than conversations? Who relates to you from a distance instead of intimately? Who prefers fear over love?

No wonder you feel afraid of God. This fear feeds off the thought of you never really knowing God and never being truly known by him. But what if there's something else behind the fear? Something more. Something far better than we could ever have hoped for or imagined.

The 2005 Oscar–winning Best Film *Crash* gives us a small glimpse of this hope. A small glimpse into God. In an intense scene toward the end of the film, Terrence

Howard's character, Cameron, finally loses it. An otherwise calm, collected, and respected individual, Cameron finally blows up after a series of events that open his eyes to the reality of racism. From being racially profiled and pulled over by the police for no crime at all, to having his wife sexually manhandled by a crooked cop (Officer Ryan, played brilliantly by Matt Dillon) right in front of his eyes, to having his life threatened by a couple of car jackers. After physically assaulting one of the car jackers and driving with him at gunpoint, Cameron attracts the attention of several police cars and a chase ensues throughout a Los Angeles suburb. The chase reaches its climax when Cameron is cornered, an otherwise good man, with a gun in his hand ready to shoot his assailant who is still in the car with him. The police are ready to fire, until a rookie cop, Officer Hanson, played by Ryan Phillippe, intercedes.

Hanson met Cameron the night before when he and Officer Ryan pulled him over. Hanson believes that Cameron is a good man in the middle of some bad choices, and he manages to position himself between the row of police with their guns aimed at Cameron. Hanson begs and pleads to his fellow officers to trust him and let Cameron go. He breaks several layers of protocol by banking his personal reputation and career on Cameron's fate. Hanson convinces his partners to back down and leave the scene as if nothing happened. As they do, Cameron is stunned and doesn't know how to take it all in. He's not sure if he should believe it or trust it. He knows what he's done. But he's being let go. His life now forever changed by an undeserved interceding act of grace.

This image is so much closer to the truth of the God we find in our moments of deep fear, shame, and guilt. Not a God who is hiding out and creeping around the corner to catch us, but rather a God who positions himself

The ~~Ten~~ Six Commandments

No doubt you've seen or heard about the Ten Commandments. You might have memorized them as a kid, seen them in one of the many Moses movies, or had them recently removed from your local courthouse. Whatever your exposure to them, the fact is that they stand for many as the bottom line of what God expects of us. If there was a *Cliff's Notes to Religion*, it would be the Ten Commandments.

Sadly, what was once understood as a gift from God has become a wall that separates us from him. Our interaction with God has been relegated to a checklist of dos and don'ts (mostly don'ts) that let us know how we're doing with God and where we're at in comparison to others. The only problem is, for some people, ten commandments just aren't enough.

If you had to rewrite the Ten Commandments based on your assumptions of God and what he expected of you, what would they be? Perhaps they're rules you learned from your parents: Thou shalt not swear (unless, of course, quoting a line from a really funny movie or repeating something Dad said while trying to fix the $%*@ lawnmower). Or from a Sunday school teacher: Thou shalt not touch your girlfriend in her "bathing suit" areas (assuming a one-piece suit, of course). Or from a teacher: Thou shalt sit still for eight hours a day, quietly conforming to everyone around you. And thou shalt always, repeat always, use a number-two pencil!

Here are a few I've picked up along the way:

1. Thou shalt not drink, smoke, or play Dungeons and Dragons ...
2. ... and thou most certainly shalt not hang out with the kids who do!
3. Thou shalt not swear, but in the case that thou dost swear, thou shalt never use the biggies (you know, like using any one of God's names as a swear word).
4. Thou shalt go to church and thou shalt act like thou likes it.
5. Thou shalt not have sex before thou art married. (It would be nice if thou didn't envy, weren't prideful, didn't have hatred in thy heart, weren't a glutton, didn't gossip, and cared for the poor and oppressed, but if thou can't do those, just make sure that thou doth not have sex before thou art married.)
6. Seriously, don't have sex.

So what would your own list look like? No matter how ridiculous your commandments might seem, it's important that you reflect on the unwritten, unspoken commandments you grew up with or learned along the way.

There's no doubt that these commandments have shaped who you are and how you interact with God. You may find yourself still following them or rebelling against them. It may even be difficult to tell the difference between the ones that are God's ideas and the ones that aren't, but it's always good to reflect on your own personal commandments. Don't brush past them as they may have a lot to tell you about who you are and who you think God is.

THERE IS NO ROOM IN LOVE FOR FEAR. WELL-FORMED LOVE BANISHES FEAR. SINCE FEAR IS CRIPPLING, A FEARFUL LIFE—FEAR OF DEATH, FEAR OF JUDGMENT—IS ONE NOT YET FULLY FORMED IN LOVE.

1 JOHN 4:18 MSG

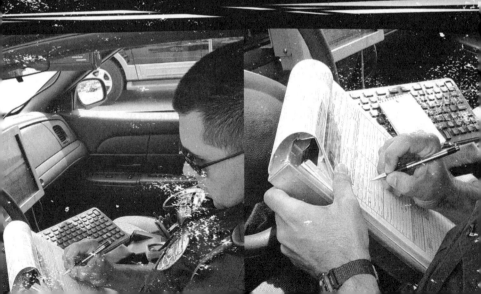

in the wide open for us to see him. A God who stands between us and the full weight and consequences of our sin and destructive habits and choices. A God who is able to uphold the law in every way, and yet still somehow make a way for us to be fully free and forgiven of all charges. We don't have to freak out or try and talk him out of busting us for what we know we've done wrong. We don't have to make excuses or make a case for why we're normally really good people. He already knows who we are. He has a rap sheet on us that could condemn us for life, he has every right to do so ... but he offers another way. A way for us to come to him instead of waiting and wondering when he will lower his final sentencing. It is the way of grace. A clearing of the record. A way that could take a lifetime to explain but only a moment to receive.

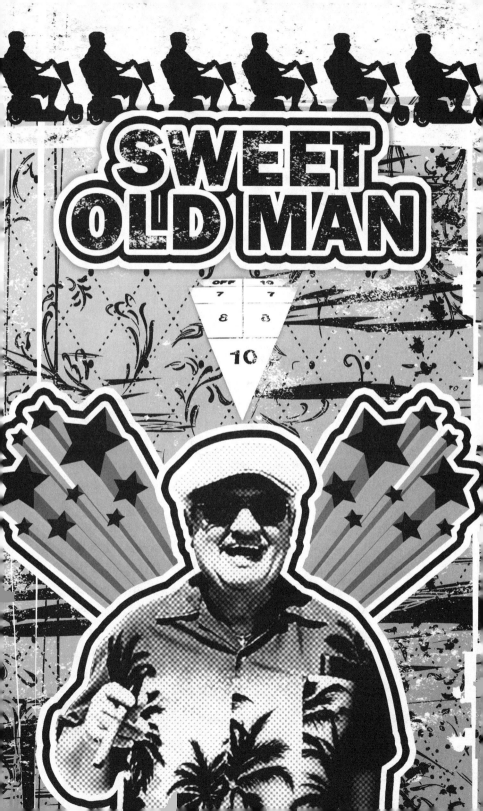

Sweet Old Man

*T*f I have to blame anyone, I guess it would be Michelangelo. I don't have anything against him personally, it's just that he has so greatly messed with our image of God. In his historic Sistine Chapel painting *The Creation of Adam*, Michelangelo masterfully crafted an image of God that I'm sure existed well before he ever picked up a brush. An image of God that continues to appear to this day on the canvas of our collective minds. The painting itself is a beautiful portrayal of God reaching out of the glory of heaven to a half-hearted, lounging Adam. God reaching out to his creation—that's a beautiful image, and I don't have a problem with that. My problem is with the actual image of God. It's just that he's so old looking. His beard, white and flowing like the fourth member of ZZ Top. His face, weatherworn. One hand reaching out to Adam, one hand reaching back for a glass of Metamucil. If there really is some sort of hidden message in da Vinci's *Mona Lisa*, then there's an obvious message in Michelangelo's *Creation*: God is old.

George Burns solidified this image in his 1977 masterpiece *Oh, God!* in which he played a cigar-toting, wisecracking, farsighted version of God. Whoever chose to cast Burns as God knew exactly what they were doing, playing into one of our most deeply rooted assumptions about God: that God loves a good stogie ... and that God is really, really old.

It's hard to imagine God any other way. Our understanding of time is so tied to our temporal existence. We cannot help but think within the construct of finality, that there is a beginning and an end. That things start and that they finish. Anything that falls outside this framework of finality gets lost in a sea of assumptions and speculations. We don't know what eternal looks like, so we try and fill in the blanks with the closest thing we have: in other words, Grandpa. Grandpa may not be eternal, but he's been around longer than any of us. And if God was here way before Grandpa ever entered the scene, God must be really old.

The Bible doesn't really help in this department either. God is referred to as the Alpha and Omega (the beginning and the end), Ageless, and Unchanging. In the Old Testament, the prophet Daniel refers to God again and again as the "Ancient of Days" (Daniel 7). All beautiful and accurate names, but names nonetheless that evoke a sense of oldness. And unlike other cultures around the world who honor, respect, and embrace their "oldness," here in America we fear old. We do everything we can to avoid it. In our culture, old is bothersome. Old is a burden. Old is out of touch. Old is not what it used to be. Old needs to be sent to live in special homes far away from the fast paced and important lives of the rest of us.

While it may be impossible to pinpoint exactly where this image of an old God came from, it's not hard to figure out where it leads. It leads us to a God who is past his prime, out of touch, over the hill, outdated, overrated, and unconnected to the world in which we live. Going back to the days of the Bible, he was moving, active, really making a name for himself. But these days, it seems as though he may have lost his edge.

Much to the protest of Christian bumper sticker writers everywhere, the fact remains that when the German philosopher Friedrich Nietzsche claimed that "God is dead," he struck a chord. But perhaps the word "dead" is a little too extreme. According to our "old man" assumptions about God, God's fate seems to have gone down a different path: God is not dead; he's actually playing shuffleboard at a retirement home somewhere in Florida.

Think about it: if God really was dead, we'd all be in trouble, but as long as God lives in a retirement community somewhere in Boca, we can have the best of both worlds.

We don't have to worry about the constant, daily, annoying presence of God; in fact, we don't even have to think about him at all if we don't want to.

And in the off chance we do want to talk to him, he's only a phone call away. We can call him every now and then when things get tough and we need someone to talk to.

We can see him whenever we want to. Maybe pay him a visit on Christmas or Easter.

We remember him at meals.

And if we are so inclined, we can even keep a picture of him up around the house or hanging from the rearview mirror.

We get our freedom, and God gets to play shuffleboard all day long.

While it's true that most of us have a decent sense of reverence and respect for the old man, few of us really believe that he's got a grip on what's going on in our world,

A Day in the Life of an Old God

4:30 a.m. — Get up before dawn (mostly because he's still responsible for the sun)

6:00 a.m. — A light and low-cholesterol breakfast while reading the paper

7:00 a.m. — Go through fan mail

12:00 p.m. — Lunch with world leaders (tentative)

1:30 p.m. — Afternoon ceramics class

3:00 p.m. — Power Pilates

4:00 p.m. — Snacks

4:30 p.m. — Shuffleboard tournament (God is currently in fourth place, but showing good game)

5:30 p.m. — Dinner with Moses, Abraham, and Elijah (this time Moses pays!)

6:30 p.m. — *Jeopardy!*

7:00 p.m. — Hang the moon

8:00 p.m. — Work on memoirs (deadlines, deadlines, deadlines!)

10:00 p.m. — Off to bed

and fewer still would be willing to bank their one and only life on a God who seems to be in the twilight of his eternity.

I've used rather frank imagery and language to describe this God, but I feel it's necessary. The destructive nature of this God is found in its subtle simplicity. It's perhaps the most visual of all the other Gods in this book. Close your eyes for a moment. You can see him, can't you? He's been there all your life, quietly corroding your impression of God. He was something great once, years ago, but now he just sits on his ancient throne watching us from a distance, too old to understand the complexity of our world, too weak to do anything about it.

The "Grand Old Man" is treated with reverence and respect — look at what a help He was to our forefathers! — but He can hardly be expected to cope with the complexities and problems of life today!

J. B. Phillips

There are too many instances in our lives where this image of an "old, weak" God damages our perceptions of who God really is.

God may have created this world, but the idea of an old God means he certainly doesn't understand it. It's too complex. He comes from a much simpler time. A time before wi-fi, before genetic engineering, before same-sex marriages, before professional wrestling. Trying to explain our world to God, the old man, is like trying to get your grandmother to listen to hip-hop. It's never gonna happen. So we lower our expectations and settle for a God who may have given us our first push, but who we passed up years ago.

God's not dead, but you'd never guess it by going to church. In fact, there are times when church feels like nothing more than a funeral service for our beloved God. Everyone dresses up and is on their best behavior, because he would have liked it that way. A pastor gets up and says something like, "Brothers and sisters, we have gathered here today to remember the Lord. For he hath done good things. In lieu of flowers, the family has requested that you put money in the basket as we pass it around, to help cover God's tab." Then you sing a song or two from an old hymnal full of words that no one uses anymore. Someone gets up and tells a story about when God did something in her life awhile back and how she'll never forget it. Then the service ends with a prayer so long you begin to wonder if you have died and gone to church. And without talking, everyone gets up and goes out to eat. With all of our remembering, our past tense verbs, and stories from thousands of years ago, it's no wonder we question whether or not God even attends church anymore.

What about the Bible? If God is nothing more than a sweet old man, then the Bible is nothing more than a big old book. A history book filled with words and stories that have little to nothing to do with the world we live in. The customs and cultures in the Bible are, for lack of a better word, ancient. Even the language reeks of oldness: "If thee thou doth partaketh in thine own folly, then thou shalt faileth thy Lord." It's like reading Shakespeare your freshman year and pretending you like it ... or even get it, when thou knoweth that thou art protesting too much and thou doesn't have a clue. We do our best to connect the dots, but there's just no getting around how dusty and difficult this book really is.

And finally, there's our everyday struggles. As long as God is an old man, our struggles are something he just doesn't understand. God obviously can't comprehend the complexity of the Internet, so he couldn't possibly understand the struggle so many face with Internet porn. His views on sexuality are so old-fashioned that it's impossible for him to understand the level of sexual addiction we face. This God is too nice to understand the anger that rages beneath the surface of our lives when someone hurts us or cuts us off while driving. God couldn't realize what you see when you look at yourself in the mirror, and there's no way he's going to be able to deal with the things you do to your body to make yourself more "acceptable." And don't even mention the things you do late at night. God's already gone to bed by the time you're just getting warmed up. How much you drink or smoke, the hidden addictions you carry, the things you watch on TV, it's all just a little too much for the old man to handle.

The longer we keep God confined to our concept of time, the older he gets. Ultimately, we can't keep thinking of God in terms of our limited and finite reality. Deep down, our hope is that he *is* a supreme being who is above all this and has power over all this and can save us from all this. That he actually is bigger, and above and beyond and before us and this whole world. The truth is, that long before us and before this world and before anything existed, there was God. That means that even before there was time, there was God. He existed outside of anything we could imagine or hope for. There was never "not God" and there never will be "not God." The Bible tells us that the night and the day, the things by which we measure time and days and months and years, were created by God. Even the time by which we falsely try to measure God was his idea.

Our limited language and perspective have greatly affected our perceptions. Perhaps a better framework for God is not "old" but "timeless." If God were limited to our understanding of time, then, like all things in this universe, he would be aging, deteriorating, dying. He couldn't be the same today as he was yesterday, or a million years ago for

EARTH AND SKY WILL WEAR OUT, BUT NOT YOU; THEY BECOME THREADBARE LIKE AN OLD COAT; YOU'LL FOLD THEM UP LIKE A WORN-OUT CLOAK, AND LAY THEM AWAY ON THE SHELF. BUT YOU'LL STAY THE SAME, YEAR AFTER YEAR; YOU'LL NEVER FADE, YOU'LL NEVER WEAR OUT.

HEBREWS 1:11–12 MSG

that matter. And he wouldn't be the same tomorrow as he is today. If he were subject to time, then he would change with time. But if time is a construct that God is not bound to, well, then that just might change everything. Because that means God loses and gains nothing, that he is perfectly complete. That means he is just as capable, just as powerful, and just as engaged and involved in our world and in our lives today as he has been throughout history.

God is still moving in and around and among us, just as he always has. God has as much love and interest in your life today as he did in the lives of Moses, Mary, Saint Peter, and your great-aunt Betty. Simply put, God is not old or young, male or female, white or black, Democrat or Republican. Those are labels and limitations, constructs and confines that we have adapted to make sense of things. But God doesn't make sense. He doesn't have to. God is so much more than the little understanding that our tiny, young minds can even possibly have. He is a boundless God who created the very minds that conceived the complexity which we hide behind. A God who cannot be shocked or caught by surprise by any aspect of your complex life. Things like terrorism, credit card debt, same-sex marriages, cloning, abortion, etc., are new to us, not to God.

It's time we put to death our good "old" God. Let the "old man" have it. Say your respects, close the casket, and walk away. This God needs to die so we can begin to see and embrace and try and keep with us a God who is not dead, but fully alive. A God who is ever present, ever active, and ever engaged in the world he created, the world he loves.

COSMIC SLOT MACHINE

Cosmic Slot Machine

I've never been to Las Vegas. Well, that's not entirely true; I've been to the Las Vegas airport several times throughout my life, which from what I understand is not all that different from going to the city itself. The Las Vegas airport stands as a modern-day testament to that bygone era known as the sixties. A time when you could walk in and out of an airport without a ticket or even the thought of a groping gate agent. A time when you could not only smoke freely in the airport, but you could actually finish your cigarette on the plane. A time when it made sense to stock an entire airport with as many slot machines as space would allow. It's like your own private casino, with the only difference being that this casino has windows, and instead of bringing you drinks every five minutes, attendants bring you peanuts. Okay, so maybe they don't bring you peanuts, but I swear to you, the place is packed with slot machines. I discovered this at the tender age of eleven, when, on a layover from a family vacation, I was able to participate in the thrill that is legalized gambling. Growing up in a religious family, I was shocked when my dad gave my brother Justin and me a handful of quarters and told us to knock ourselves out. And "knock ourselves out" we did!

There is a primal drive that emerges in the presence of gambling. Something tells you that despite the odds, despite the level of chance, despite the fact that people have destroyed their entire lives in a matter of mere moments in a casino, that somehow, you're a winner. Having grown up on video games and Chuck E. Cheese's tokens, the concept of a slot machine didn't take long for me to grasp. Put your money in, pull the shiny lever, and wait to see if the cartoon fruits match up. If one of these fruits is not like the other, you lose. But if all three match ... cha ching!

We watched my dad as he systematically made his way from slot machine to slot machine. Some people sat on their ratty vinyl stools for hours, attempting to break the machine down by a sheer act of gambling will. But not my dad. After about four or five pulls, he would move on to the next, and then the next, and then the next. It's as though he knew them, as if he had been here before. He spoke to them in hushed tones reminiscent of the Horse Whisperer, telling them exactly what he wanted them to do. It was working. Every ten pulls, he won. Sometimes big, sometimes small. It didn't even faze him. It's like he knew he was going to win.

Meanwhile, I watched with my palm still clenched around my quarters, which were now sweating along with me in nervous anticipation. I waited and debated and eventually gave in. There's nothing like the rush of underage gambling, especially underage airport gambling. While I don't remember winning much, I do remember the intense feeling of exhilaration that comes from gambling, and the confidence that comes from gambling with someone else's money.

I haven't gambled much since then. The closest I get is eBay. But I do have a friend who gambles often and is quite good. In my opinion, he's gifted in the ways of gambling. He can leave his house at 11:00 p.m. with $100 and return at 2:00 a.m. with anywhere from $500 to $1,200! There's only one catch though: the guy is a pastor! Which raises a few questions. Isn't there some sort of conflict of interest here? Does he pray before he rolls? Does he have to tithe on something like that? And is it possible that he is, in fact, guided by the very hand of God? A modern-day Joan of Arc at the craps table.

At the Christian college I went to, I had to sign an agreement that I wouldn't use "face cards" (I wasn't even sure what those were), so we took the game "Pass the Pigs" and figured out a way to gamble on that. I believe there is a very spiritual component to gambling. Stupid, but spiritual.

There is on one hand, the type of gambling Jesus endorsed. The type where we lay our lives on the line in an act of faith before God. That sort of risky "bet the farm" kind of faith is hands down the best gamble a person can make. But there's another side to the coin. One that lives not out of faith, but rather with crossed fingers. It's a life that has little to do with love and everything to do with luck. It's an approach to God and all things spiritual as a sort of cosmic crapshoot. It goes something like this:

You pull into the mall parking lot on a Saturday afternoon and the place is packed. As you begin to settle in for an hour-long expedition to find a spot, you notice a space, not ten feet from the mall entrance. You pull in, feeling a small but sure sense of blessedness. You win!

You're running late for a flight (an experience I would know nothing about, but I have friends who have explained the process to me). There's still a slim chance you could

How to Gamble
the Christian College Way

Pass the Pigs

If you roll a...	You will get...
Razorback	5 points
Double Razorback	20 points
Trotter	5 points
Double Trotter	20 points
Snouter	10 points
Double Snouter	40 points
Leaning Jowler	15 points
Double Leaning Jowler	60 points
Pig Out	0 points
Sider	1 point
Oinker	Back to zero
Mixed Combo	Combined score

Scoring information from
www.pugetsoundwa.net/playland/pigs.html.

get to the airport on time if everything goes your way. Traffic is rough, but you make it with only minutes to spare. Now all you have to do is get through security with no hassles. It takes longer than you had hoped, namely because the guy in front of you decided to make a joke about having an explosive tip toothbrush in his carry-on. You make it to the gate seconds after they close it ... only to learn that the next flight to Rochester doesn't leave for another six hours. You lose.

Let's raise the spiritual stakes a little bit. In the Bible you read about hundreds of people whom Jesus miraculously healed of just about every disease under the sun. People who had been confined to rotting bed mats their entire lives are suddenly up on their feet dancing. People who had been ostracized from society in every way are now honored guests at the table of acceptance. They win. But what of the thousands of people whom Jesus didn't heal? What of those who suffered just as severely, who traveled miles for the chance that they too might be healed ... but were not? Not because Jesus couldn't, but because he didn't. Do they lose? What about those people who live like hell their entire lives, and on their deathbeds, pray a prayer to get into heaven? Do they win? And what about the millions upon millions of good people who bet their lives on a certain religion only to die and find out they picked the wrong one? Do they lose?

=====

*[This God] can move in a mysterious way,
or an outrageous way, or an unjust way, his wonders
to perform; and no one can say him nay.*

J. B. Phillips

=====

After hundreds of years of living with the mystery of God, it's no wonder many have written life and God off as one big gamble. Despite desire, despite good behavior, despite others winning all around you, you don't win. You don't get what you came for. Making sense of that can be exhausting, frustrating, and downright heartbreaking. So maybe it's true that life, and God, for that matter, are like a cosmic slot machine: you win some, you lose some. And the best you can hope for is to break even in the end and to leave the table with nothing more than what you walked in with.

For most of my life I've been aware of the reality of God. And for equally as long I have been perplexed as to how and why things work out the way they do. I've wondered why some people seem to skate through life while others are dragged through it kicking and screaming. Or why everything seems to go right for some people while others are drawn to hard times like a magnet in a junkyard. I've watched as some people have had no problem finding the person of their dreams while others fall into bad relationship after bad relationship. I don't understand why some babies are born perfectly healthy while others are born with physical and mental disabilities that will affect them the rest of their lives. Why does the lot of one's life come down to something so simple and out of control as the color of their skin, their gender, the country they were born in, the family they're born into?

This questioning can easily lead to one of several conclusions:

- God is involved in every detail and has a reason for everything, even though it might be beyond our understanding.

- God is biased, and the "blessed" and "cursed" are living proof.

- God is random, and what you get is what you get. What you do with it is up to you.

None of these conclusions sits particularly well with me. But the one that's been easiest for me to live with has definitely been the last one—that God is basically good, but utterly random and beyond my control. The only option we have is to suck it up and play the cards we've been dealt. Don't get me wrong. I would love for it to be different; I hope beyond hope that it's different, but the wins and losses of my life would tell another story.

The seeming randomness of God led me to believe at a young age that you should always hedge your bets and play it safe, or you could lose it all. I saw it all around me. Despite our parents doing the best they could with us kids, the truth is that some of us had a difficult go at life while others of us didn't. When it came to me, my parents decided to play the odds and pay the cost for me to have a religious education, and although I am extremely grateful, it only seemed to entrench the sense of randomness I perceived in God. Kids still partied, still got high, still got pregnant, and of the forty-eight graduates from my senior class, I would bet that around half are still interested in God.

When it came to dating, I would only go after the girls that I thought were sure bets. Through a complex mathematical equation involving likeability (L) times hotness (H) times availability (A) divided by the guts (G) I had to ask them out, I determined (with great accuracy) who would be my next girlfriend. (Again, that's LHA/G = girlfriend.) None of this, "Do you like me, check one of the following boxes" business. That was for amateurs.

When it came to choosing a college, instead of taking the gamble of applying to the schools I might want to go to, only to face the greater odds of being rejected, I went to a local college where just about everyone gets accepted. A place that was just like high school, only with ashtrays.

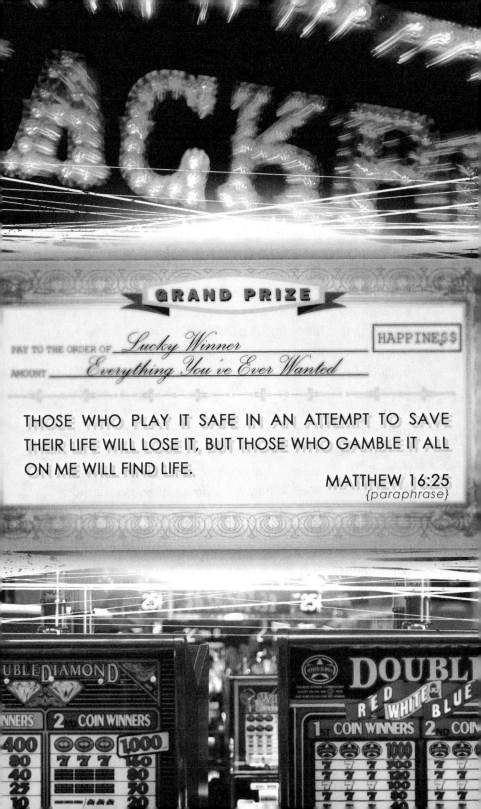

For most of my life I've tried playing it safe, settling for the nickel slots of destiny, never winning big, but most important, never losing it all. With all my might I've tried to contain the randomness of God the best I could, but to no avail. Girls still broke my heart, friends still hurt me, loved ones still died, and God still seemed to act however he wanted.

Even as I write these words I'm sitting on the patio of an absolutely beautiful Mexican resort ... and it's raining (cue Alanis Morissette). Jeanne and I have come here to rest, reflect, and dream. We come here from one of the most random years of our lives. It started with the sudden death of Jeanne's father, Bill. A man who was in better shape than any of us died of a heart attack and poor medical attention while running in a race with his son Eddie. Four months after his death, the family put on suits and ties once more to celebrate the marriage of Jeanne's little brother, Eddie, to his wife Leah. Two months after that, I was asked to officiate the funerals of three former students from the high school ministry Jeanne and I used to work in. They all died of separate causes, all within three weeks of each other. Yet, through every one of those funerals, I knew a secret. That even in the presence of such death, there was a little life growing inside my wife's tummy. Ironically enough, our first child was conceived somewhere between a wedding and a funeral.

I wonder how the odds have fared for you in your life. Perhaps it's been a story of wins. Perhaps losses. Probably somewhere in between. Odds are though, that however you have fared, it's greatly affected your opinion and perception of God. If you have come out ahead so far, then it's probably not all that hard for you to trust God (besides, it seems like he's on your side). If it feels like you've had more losses than wins, then it is fair to assume you are reserved when it comes to trusting God, reluctant at best. You have to wonder where God is every time you win or lose in your life. What is God's involvement in every blessing, every catastrophe, every good day, every bad day, every great parking spot, every failed relationship, and so on? Is it all just random? Is it all his doing? These are questions (and answers) that shape us more than we know.

It was when my father-in-law Bill died that I saw just how varied people's opinions are on the subject of God's role in the details of our lives. Some people joined in our heavenward rage and questioning. Others stood silent. Still others told us that this was all a part of God's bigger plan. As if that was supposed to bring some comfort. If I heard one more person tell me that it was Bill's time, so help me, I was going to punch them in the teeth. To be honest, there were several months when all I wanted was to punch God in the teeth (I don't even know if God has teeth, but I'm thankful he never stopped loving me while I was swinging). Death stirs these questions up fast: Did God make it happen? Did he allow it to happen? Was God as surprised as I was? Everyone seemed willing to offer their advice on the subject, but few gave me the answers I was really looking for. Somewhere along the way, I gave up on answers and moved to longing. I longed to know that God at least fell somewhere between random and responsible. That the odds in this life are not "controlled by the house" (God) but the direct effects of sin and free will. I finally accepted that I will never understand where God is at in all of the wins and losses of my life, and I simply longed to know he was with me. Whether or not he was surprised or right on schedule was inconsequential to me. I longed to know that he was sad with me. That he would stay with me. This is the God I longed for, and ultimately the God that I am finding and putting my faith in.

I could take the rest of this book to try and explain how it all works and where God is in all of it, but I would be left with a loss of definitive words. No one definitively knows how God works. But I do know this: of every person I have ever known and of every story I have ever read in the Bible, those who play it safe and hedge their bets on life never really live it; those who hedge their bets on God never really know him.

A glance through the stories in the Bible shows a spread of wins and losses. Abraham was invited to gamble his fertility (or lack thereof) on God, and lo and behold, God gave him a nation. Joseph was invited to bet his faith and integrity and won the role of Secretary of State of Egypt, one of the most powerful nations in the known world. Ruth was invited to roll the dice on trusting God to provide love and security once again, and she walked away with Boaz. Saul was invited to place his bets on God's power versus his own, but sadly bet on himself and lost everything that mattered to him.

A young teenage girl bets her reputation and her very body on the promise of the Messiah and wins. A bunch of working class fishermen bet everything on Jesus, while a rich young ruler lowered his head and walked away from the table. These stories of wins and losses go on to this very day.

It's no different for you and me. There is an invitation, a risky opportunity that God has given you. Will you take that handful of quarters you call faith and place your bet on God? The choice is yours. He gives you no guarantee that you won't be hurt or suffer or even take some losses, but he does promise you this: he loves you, he knows you, he is with you, and *you will win*. Everyone who has ever bet their one and only life on God always wins. Cha ching indeed.

Talent Show Judge

9.5 | 10 | 9

For as long as there have been people with even the slightest shred of dignity, there have been people who are there to tear them apart. It's inevitable, almost Darwinian. The human species is so hungry for approval that we will do almost anything to gain that primal sense of acceptance. It's nothing new. Long before *American Idol*, long before *Star Search*, long before Amateur Night at the Apollo; there was of course the school talent show.

The idea of the talent show is quite beautiful. The idea of people believing they have a unique talent, skill, or ability is beautiful. The assumption that their talent, skill, or ability should be recognized, even celebrated, is beautiful. The diversity of what we consider "talent," is beautiful. Everything about it is beautiful.

The mechanics of the talent show are really quite simple. It starts with the naive and beautiful belief that you, the little snowflake that you are, have a unique talent, skill, or ability. That you, in fact, are special. But you knowing that you are special is not quite enough. Others need to know. You need to put your uniqueness on the line. So you submit your uniqueness to an anonymous table of experts who supposedly know what is talent and what is not, what is special and what is not, what is good and what is not. Unfortunately, more often than not, what you hear is that while your rendition of Whitney Houston's, "Greatest Love of All" was good, it just wasn't good enough. And you are forced to face not only your own rejection, but the celebration and exaltation of those around you who are "good enough."

The modern high-pressure Christian of certain circles would like to impose perfection of one hundred per cent as a set of rules to be immediately enforced, instead of as a shining ideal to be faithfully pursued.

J. B. Phillips

What makes something so beautiful and straightforward end up so terrifying and painful? Simple—the talent show judge.

You can see it now in the back of your subconscious, packed away to protect you. They sit there behind that eight-foot-long folding table, clipboards in hand, whispering and mumbling back and forth between each other, offering the barest minimum of words—"thank you" and "next." Talent show judges. Who do they think they are? Who are they to judge me on whether or not my version of "Greatest Love of All" is worthy of the Thomas Jefferson Middle School auditorium stage? Who are they to tell me that my dramatic interpretation of Song of Solomon, chapter 4 isn't what they had in mind for the school speech meet? And since when is drinking the Oreo and toothpaste backwash of ten of my friends not considered a talent?

In my opinion, it is the rejection of the talent show judge that gave way to the birth of karaoke. Aside from

Seven "Talents" You Are Guaranteed to See at Almost Every Talent Show

1. At least one, if not several, Whitney Houston songs (if you're lucky, they'll be in a medley).
2. At least one, if not several, boys swapping backwash, feeding each other like a momma bird and baby bird, performing inappropriate stunts, and kicking each other in places boys shouldn't be kicked. (I would like to take this moment to personally apologize on behalf of all boys everywhere. I am sorry. We are boys. That's what we do.)
3. Someone struggling through a Dave Matthews song (most likely "Satellite").
4. A "comedian" whose jokes about the South are not only not funny, but potentially racist.
5. An interpretive dance (accompanied by a cassette tape).
6. A declaration of love made by an otherwise quiet fifteen-year-old kid, his guitar, and an original song he wrote for Ami Walker titled "I'll Walk with You."
7. Eight minutes of talent, eighty-two minutes of uncomfortable and unforgettable fun.

church, karaoke is the place where all the kids who weren't good enough for the talent show go to share their "talent" with the world. Karaoke gives you all of the essential ingredients that were absent at your talent show audition:

Better music selection

Lyrics

Background vocals

An audience with incredibly low standards

The absence of a judge

Why anyone would willingly submit their precious snowflake self to the white-hot rejection of something like a talent show is beyond me. Why anyone would choose that for themselves is a mystery. And yet, for many, that is precisely the life they have chosen. A life of endless attempts at impressing a distant and difficult-to-please God. A life of perpetual performance and feelings of regular rejection. A life of memorizing lines, learning cues, playing a part, all for the slim chance of winning the elusive approval of a God who might by some slim chance find one "good enough."

There is a word whispered into the exhausted ear of those who choose to give in to the demands of the talent show judge. That word is "more." More. The mere hint of it both demands and defeats. More. "That was good, but not good enough." More. The promise of perfection dangling inches away from a treadmill of good works and good intentions. More. There is more to learn. There is more to do. There is more to read. There is more to give. In our sad and holy attempt to follow God, we destroy the very life he supposedly came to save. You see it in churches where guilt and obligation flow mingled down from pleading pulpits—smiling small group leaders, sweat-drenched parking team recruiters, tenured Sunday school teachers, outdated missionary family photos, and empty but expectant offering plates. There is always something more to do at church. Another class opens up, another need arises, another building needs to be built, another starving child needs to be sponsored. More.

This is a concept all too familiar with anyone who has grown up in the church. You see it in the bulletin. Sunday is divided between the traditional service at 8:00 a.m., the contemporary service at 10:00 a.m., the new conditional service at 12:00 p.m. (a mission-minded fusion of the contemporary service with the traditional service), and has the day rounding to a close at 8:13 p.m. with the Emergent service (if you have to ask who that's for, then it's clearly not for you). Monday morning gets off to an early start with the 5:00 a.m. men's breakfast and the 6:00 a.m. women's Bible study titled "Women Doing Life Together" (surprisingly, not a small group of ex-cons). Tuesday night is the Christian Couples Cooking Class (CCCC for short). Wednesday is "Drop the kids off and go to a movie" night. Thursday is the all-church prayer meeting from 10:45 a.m. to 11:20 a.m. Thursday night is a flurry of drama, dance, puppet, and vocal team rehearsals, with a volleyball league thrown in for good measure. Friday night is when the marriage ministry pulls out all the stops with a wide assortment of premarital counseling classes, marriage workshops, and cheap if not free "date nights." And the week winds to a close on Saturday with the annual all day seminar on time management. More.

You see it in the inner recesses of your own personal life. There is always more you can do with your business practices to honor God. There is more you can do with your finances. There are always more books to read, more time you should be spending in prayer, more chapters to read in the Bible, more friends to bring to church, more "bad" stuff to cut out of your life, more catchphrases to incorporate into your spiritual lexicon. More.

You see it among parents, who despite their best and worst efforts, still can't seem to raise their kids God's way. There are always new and more godly methods to raising your kids, more prayers you should be praying for your kids, new books to tell you what God would do with your kids if he were you, and other families who seem to get it all right (and who never seem to be shy in letting you know it). More.

You don't have to be religious to recognize it. You feel it late at night, watching images of starving African kids tucked in between ads for beer and 900 numbers. You should really do something for those kids. You feel it when a neighbor asks you to go to church with them, and you realize that since the last time you went to church, your oldest child has not only learned to walk, but to drive. You really should go to church more. You feel it when your $140 shoes have to step over another homeless person downtown. You really should do something for the less fortunate. You can feel it just about anywhere you go or in anything you do.

Keeping up with the constant call for "MORE" can be overwhelming and exhausting. It requires a full-time commitment with a willingness to work nights and weekends. Why do so many people lose themselves in the soul-suffocating quicksand of more? And more important, who is it that keeps asking for more?

At the church my wife used to attend, there was an older couple who had spent the majority of their lives following God the Talent Show Judge. They had answered the cosmic demand for more. They had done it all, and then some. They had been missionaries, pastors, conference speakers, authors, hosts of a national radio program, and board members of some of the most prestigious evangelical organizations in the world. Not only had they done more than most, they had done it better than most. Everybody respected them, while few actually ever knew them. They were the model of what it meant to live Christianlike. If anyone deserved to hear "Well done" from God, it was them.

And yet I sometimes wonder that if God were to tell them "Well done," whether they would even recognize his still, small voice. For while they did more for God than most, it seemed as though they knew him less and less. Religion for God had eclipsed relationship with God until their inner lives were lost to their outer lives. Those who knew them well, knew them to be little more than well-fortified facades. The strong, sturdy shell of godliness without its gentle growing grace. Somewhere along the way they substituted activity for intimacy, and the rest is history. The legacy they gave their children and grandchildren left little to be desired. Forced to grow up in the midst of trying to keep up with their parents, their children did the best they could to put the pieces together of a God that nearly tore their family apart. They stand as monuments to me of how hard one can try and still completely miss the point. Of how there is a Grand Canyon–sized gap between busyness and godliness, intimacy and insanity.

I am all too familiar with this talent show judge of a God. I was introduced to him in my early twenties. It began when I moved to Chicago in the unmercifully hot summer of 1995. I was so excited to finish up my final year of college (my fifth year on a four-year plan). I was recently engaged to Jeanne and we were caught up in all the excitement of planning our wedding. I scored a job as a doorman in Chicago's Gold Coast neighborhood, opening doors and

I'M AFTER LOVE THAT LASTS, NOT MORE RELIGION.
I WANT YOU TO KNOW GOD, NOT GO TO MORE
PRAYER MEETINGS.

HOSEA 6:6 MSG

GOING THROUGH THE MOTIONS DOESN'T PLEASE YOU,
A FLAWLESS PERFORMANCE IS NOTHING TO YOU. I
LEARNED GOD-WORSHIP WHEN MY PRIDE WAS
SHATTERED. HEART-SHATTERED LIVES READY FOR LOVE
DON'T FOR A MOMENT ESCAPE GOD'S NOTICE.

PSALM 51:16–17 MSG

carrying groceries for the last remnant of Chicago's "old money." It was an exhilarating time. One of my academic requirements was to volunteer four hours a week in a local church or inner-city ministry. I decided to volunteer at a church in the suburbs, called Willow Creek. Willow at that time averaged around twenty thousand people attending each week. Finding four hours of volunteer work would be a breeze. Little did I know what I was in for. My first clue should have been a little blue 8½ x 11 sheet of paper that broke down the requirements and expectations for volunteering in the high school ministry. To be a responsible volunteer meant six hours of setup, attendance, and teardown for our big Tuesday night student outreach program. Then there was the Wednesday afternoon two-hour leadership meeting, the hour-and-a-half Wednesday evening small group I was in, followed by two hours of church on Wednesday night. Friday nights were given to football games, chaperoning school dances, and of course, serving as the driver for many elicit late night TPing sessions. Sunday afternoon brought two more hours of a small group that I led, followed by a three-hour setup, attendance, and teardown of our Sunday night student worship service. Once you added in all the camps, retreats, and late night "I can't believe she just broke up with me" phone calls, I was clocking in around twenty hours a week at church alone—all as a volunteer. Somewhere in there (I think it was Mondays ... or was it Thursdays ...) I went to school, worked, and fulfilled my duties as a fiancé.

And while I loved every minute of it (all 1,247 minutes each week), I realize now that I was driven by a word that was not heard but felt—more. Everything I was doing was wonderful, but there was always more. There were more meetings, more students to pick up after school, more parents who wanted me to fix their kids, more opportunities to dive into. Somehow, the more I did, the more it felt like it was never quite enough. Again, no one ever said this to me directly. They didn't have to. It's just an assumption I had about God and what he wanted, buried deep within my overextended soul.

Without realizing it, we have carelessly created for ourselves a God whom we can never please. It is a God who keeps us busy with endless activity and piety without purpose. A God who is never impressed. Why would we ever do such a thing? Who in their right mind would create, let alone submit themselves to, such a God? Maybe it has something to do with the Western myth of busyness. We live in a culture that reveres busyness. Busyness and activity exist as our way of cleverly covering up our cluelessness. No one wants to admit we don't know what to do when it comes to God, so we begin to do anything and everything we think he might want. The more we do, the more we look like we know what we're doing, all the while never really knowing the one we're attempting to do it all for.

We are all born with a deep desire to please God, housed in the flesh and bone of human limitation. It's a good desire. I believe it is a God-given desire. One that can either be unleashed through a hand-in-hand relationship with the true God or crushed under the foot of religious guilt and obligation. For there is a thin line between pleasing and performing. Pleasing lives and thrives in the dynamic of delight—God delighting in you, you delighting in God. This is what you were created for. Performing, on the other hand, is held captive by demand. Your attempts to please God are never good enough. There is always more. And over time, the more you cease to sense God's inexplicable delight in you, the more your life begins to resemble a sad series of talent show auditions, ever hoping to impress or earn what was already offered to you.

You see, the great tragedy of all this drama is that when you do finally work yourself into the inevitable exhaustion that comes from trying to impress God, and you fall off your little stage, you will find that seated at that dark and demanding table of judges is not at all who you expected. It is not the Talent Show God of More, but you and I who are seated there, demanding and expecting ourselves to live up to, to impress, to earn what God had already offered long before we ever set about putting together our act. Tragically, it is not God, but you and I who demand and defeat and call out for more and more. It is our own ungodly expectations that meet with our own human limitations to create the conflict we so often find ourselves in. God is not the nameless, faceless, unpleased judge in the back of our minds. He is in fact the one (sometimes the only one) cheering us on. For some this is far more shocking than the God of More. So defeated and depleted are we from all of our activity for God that we can hardly hear or recognize the delight of God when it fills the auditorium hall. Even though it is what we so deeply desire, it is not what we have come to expect. His cheers ring out not for our flawless performances, but for our sheer existence. He loves us and delights in us not because of what we do for him, but because of who we are to him. It is from this place of love and acceptance that I long to serve God, not the other way around. Not even our best rendition of "Greatest Love of All" can earn us what is already being offered to us. Maybe ... if you stopped performing ... for just one minute ... you might hear it too.

All-You-Can-Eat Buffet

I'm always a little surprised when I see statistics that say 90 percent of Americans believe in God. This percentage seems unrealistically higher than anything our culture is capable of. My hunch is that if you probed a little deeper and asked these 90 percent of Americans just who exactly is their God, things would get a little fuzzy. My belief is that most of the people who say they believe in God are good and sincere people who genuinely do believe in some form of God or another, with the largest percentage worshiping a God that encompasses a buffet of beliefs.

For a percentage of people, this God takes on the vague form of nothingness. He ... she ... it ... resembles more of an idea than a person. If this God took any shape, it would be a sort of ambiguous, ambivalent cloud. A God who lacks any sense of flavor. Devoid of dynamic personality or distinguishing features. It has no emotions, no opinions, and exists ultimately outside of relationship. It's a God for those who don't really want to have to think about God too much. More thought, detail, and attention is given to the imaginary friends of our childhood than to this God.

It's a God for those who don't feel the need to interact with him ... her ... it. It's hard to have a bad experience with this God; in fact, it's hard to have any sort of experience at all. This is a God who takes up little space in our minds and even less space in our souls. This is the God of vague nothingness.

For many others though, God takes on the vague form of "everythingness," a sort of catchall for our divine assumptions. The God of the all-you-can-eat buffet. There is perhaps no more American an idea than that of the all-you-can-eat buffet. It offers us the one thing we love most—more. If you want a chimichanga, you can have it. If you want spaghetti, you can have it. If you want a baked potato smothered in peanut butter and hollandaise, you can have it.

If the all-you-can-eat buffet is the epitome of the American ideal, then my dad is the most patriotic man to walk the face of the earth. He approaches the buffet like a man on a mission. It's personal to him. When our family went on our first (and last) cruise together, my dad hit the buffet like it was the whole point of the trip. Sure there were sights to be seen, two-dollar T-shirts to be purchased, and hair to be braided, but all he was interested in was the buffet. Not only was he enamored with the spread, but he was genuinely taken aback with the open-ended availability. For this was no ordinary buffet, no, this was a twenty-four-hour buffet. Four words that should never inhabit the same sign—*twenty-four-hour buffet*. All my dad saw was "everything" "always." That's all he needed. By the end of our cruise, you could bounce a quarter off that man's belly. It was taut.

But the "all-you-can-eat apple" doesn't fall far from the tree. I too am a lover of the utopian idea of the buffet. I see it as my own form of consumer justice for all the overpriced

Nine Items You Should Always Pass On at the All-You-Can-Eat Buffet

1. Anything with the word "surprise" in it
2. The egg rolls (a mistake I make every time)
3. Szechuan pizza
4. Any one of the many potpies that are available
5. The ham loaf
6. The Catch of the Day (the words "catch" and "day" should always be suspect)
7. Shepherd's pie
8. The tuna enchilada
9. Anything that looks like, smells like, or contains trace elements of tapioca

meals I've ever eaten. It's my small way of sticking it to the man. I will break the buffet system and make them rethink their open-ended policy. That's why I love the buffet. That and the fact that I am supremely cheap.

It was only a matter of time. We are a culture inundated and overwhelmed with options. And in the natural progression of things (or digression depending on your perspective), we as a people have moved from being customers to being customizers. Look around you—it's all about you. From the way you shop and what you shop for, to your new MC Hammer ringtone, to the 4,173 songs on your iPod, to the words you use when you order a cup of coffee. (Did we even know what "macchiato" meant before Starbucks told us that we needed it?) We have found ways of making almost everything around us somehow about us. So it should come as no surprise that we would even find a way to customize God.

I remember sitting in a coffee shop a few years back and having a conversation with Sam, an employee there. After watching me come in week after week and sitting in the corner with my headphones on, banging away on my laptop, Sam got up the nerve to ask me what it was that I was working on. When I told him I was a pastor and that I was working on my message for the weekend, the conversation took an unexpectedly interesting turn. Sam decided to take his thirty-minute break with me. He came back to the table where I was working, and over a grande skim, chai tea latte, no foam, no water, two pumps extra chai, we talked about all things faith. Sam asked which faith system I ascribed to (a question that sounded more clinical than spiritual). After trying to explain to him that I am more like a non-denominational free agent, I decided that "Jesus follower" was the easiest and most specific definition for him to wrap his head around. I asked him what he believes, and more specifically, who he believes. Sam went into an answer that went way over his thirty-minute break. He told me his story, a story of religious disillusionment as a child, of divine avoidance as a teenager, and eventual spiritual discovery and experimentation as a college student. He told me how he had come to discover the beauty in all faiths and that he refused to be labeled or confined to any one system of beliefs. He explained how Christianity taught him about faith in general, how Buddhism had taught him to meditate each day, and how hybrid, New-Age philosophies had opened his eyes to his connectedness to the world around him. His understanding and explanation of what he believed was clear and sincere. But when I asked him who he believed in, his answer revealed far more than the last thirty minutes of his story. His answer was simple and to the point—"I believe in me." The elaborate system of his faith all boiled down to one simple fact—that in the end, he had created a faith around himself. There was nothing "bigger than" or "greater than" calling him to anything other than himself. For all his picking and choosing of faith, he was still left with nothing more than the very thing he started with—himself.

We continued meeting for the next couple of months to have spiritual conversations, until eventually he moved to another store. I went back to my corner, headphones on, banging away on my computer, but I couldn't stop thinking about my conversations with Sam. Our conversations revealed an idea that is at the very core of this chapter—that it's possible to spend your whole life filling your plate with your favorite parts about God, while your soul slowly starves from divine malnourishment.

This smorgasbord of spirituality is how so many people like their God—a buffet, a hodgepodge, a veritable cornucopia of all the things we like in a deity, and none of the things we don't. A plate overflowing with all the best parts. A God who encompasses the grace of Christianity, with the meditation practices of Eastern religions, with a dash of Catholic ritual, and a smidge of "health and wealth" to top it all off. Incongruity is no issue so long as you don't think about it for too long. Continuity only complicates when there are clearly parts you just don't like and don't want on your plate.

> *The trouble with many people today is that they have not found a God big enough for modern needs.*
>
> *J. B. Phillips*

For my thirtieth birthday, my best friend blew me away with a surprise visit. He gave me a birthday gift I would never have given myself. He and his wife, Stephanie, took Jeanne and me out for the most incredible meal of my life. He somehow got us reservations at the world renowned Charlie Trotter's restaurant in Chicago. The waiting list at Trotter's is typically two to three months long, and Shadd got us in the day before. Only God and Oprah can get you in on that short of notice. Charlie Trotter's is one of those unique dining experiences that is far better experienced than explained, but I'll do my best.

First of all, there are no prices on the menu. This is never a good sign. You really don't know what you're in for until the very end. (I suggest taking out a small loan up front, just to be safe.) Second, the entire meal is a process. Since it was a seven-course meal, the whole experience lasted well over three hours. Every course building off of the previous, all of it perfectly prepared and displayed, in its proper place and at the perfect time. Third, you really must eat everything. There's just no place to be picky. Every course of the meal is contingent on the previous, all of it building to the perfect crescendo. And with the average bite coming in right around five dollars a forkful, you can't afford not to eat it. At that birthday meal we dined on "Razor Clams and Wellfleet Oysters with Heirloom Tomato Water, Maine Diver Scallop with Thai Eggplant, and Grass-fed Veal Loin with Lobster Mushrooms." We topped it all off with "Raw Tahitian Vanilla Bean Ice Cream with Red Michigan Raspberries." It was hands down the most perfect dining experience I've ever had and a memory I will never forget. (Note to my friends: when dining at Charlie Trotter's, keep in mind that an 18 percent gratuity is already added. Do not make the generous mistake that Shadd made by tipping on top of that. It's an error that could keep your kids from going to college.)

The genius of an experience like Charlie Trotter's is that it forced me to submit to foods I've never even heard of and may never eat again. I'm not a big fish guy, but I ate every slippery bite of my razor clams and Wellfleet oysters because I didn't want to miss a thing. The worth and importance of each bite outweighed my picky preferences. I trusted that Charlie knew and cared more about my taste buds than any part-time employee at the Old Country Buffet, and because of this blind trust I was saved from another bland and boring meal. I truly was given a gift.

OPEN YOUR MOUTH AND TASTE, OPEN YOUR EYES AND SEE—HOW GOOD GOD IS. BLESSED ARE YOU WHO RUN TO HIM.

PSALM 34:8 MSG

This is the gift of putting your faith in the one true God. There are dishes that are downright delightful and perfectly pleasing. And then there are courses you would much rather skip. But it all has to be taken in to have the gift of the meal as it was intended, a meal that is far better experienced than explained.

Could it be that in your desire to pick the best parts of everything, you have been left with the very worst part of nothingness? A bland and boring menu of beliefs that exists only within the confines of your own personal preferences? A faith that calls nothing out of you and ultimately gives you nothing in return? Maybe this is why 90 percent of Americans say they believe in God, because they only believe in about 10 percent of him.

Real faith comes from releasing control and choosing the whole of God instead of fabricating a God of your favorite parts. God is inseparably whole. He cannot be divided and portioned out into the parts we find most palatable. He is who he is, all of who he is. And he is inviting you to be the same. All of who you are, following all of who God is. The table has been set, the meal lovingly prepared. Will you join us and dine from the fullness of God's table?

YOUR PARENTS

SUPER-SIZED

Your Parents . . . Supersized

It's Thursday at 11:37 a.m. and I'm on the phone with Shadd. This is not an uncommon occurrence. Shadd has one of those jobs where he can call me at 11:37 a.m. and think nothing of it. So there we were at 11:37 a.m. talking on the phone about different approaches to disciplining a child. Not a typical conversation for two guys in their thirties to have at any time of day. But that's how Shadd and I are. It makes a little bit more sense in light of the fact that Shadd is the father of a two-year-old son. A son he named after me of all people: Jarrett Hudson Williams. I vividly remember receiving Shadd's elated phone call from the hospital lobby just moments after Jarrett was born, as he told me the name he had chosen for his first son. I can't fully explain to you what an honor that is. Little Jarrett, living up to his namesake and living up to all the stereotypes of a two-year-old boy, is incessantly active. In light of that, Shadd and his wife Stephanie have had to create and adapt a clear and consistent system of discipline. Which brings me back to our phone call.

Shadd says to me in the middle of our conversation, unaware of the weight of his words, that every time he disciplines Jarrett, he realizes he is shaping and reinforcing Jarrett's perception of God. In other words, Little Jarrett's big picture of God is being immediately and indelibly formed with every interaction he has with his parents. This is no small thing.

As I write these words I am about eight weeks away from becoming a father myself (give or take our baby's own personal schedule). When you finally read these words I will already be several pages into this exciting and overwhelming chapter of my life. At the same time, as I write these words, I am in the spiritual process of unpacking and understanding how my parents, in good and bad ways, shaped and reinforced *my* perception of and experience with God. And finally, as you read these words, I am aware that I will have already penned the first few frail lines of my own child's perception of and experience with God. Good or bad, like it or not, the bottom line is that there is no more powerful force in the universe that shapes your perception of and experience with God outside of your parents.

The thought of it all seemed so cliché the first time I sat across from my counselor. But there he was, walking me through my childhood and connecting the dysfunctional dots back to my parents. It was equal parts predictable and powerful as it sent me on a five-year journey that has now picked up intensity as I prepare to be a parent myself. How have my parents negatively and positively shaped my perception of God? It's an important question to be sure. It's a question not of *if*, but of *how*.

Perhaps you may be thinking, "Is this going to be another one of those autobiographical pity parties that does nothing more than justify my current state of brokenness by blaming the mistakes in my parents' past?" Unfortunately, it's not ... but that *would* be fun! This is nothing more than me looking for the glimpses of God (be they broken or beautiful) in the truth of my story. It's not an attempt to slam my parents or exact some kind of revenge on them for grounding me from my girlfriend for the entire summer between my junior and senior years of high school. The truth is, I have wonderful parents and am truly grateful to God for them. They have seen these words before you. We have talked about the meaning behind them and are working together to build new paradigms of love for the family that Jeanne and I have started. Now that that's out of the way, let's get to the dirt!

At four years old, an image of God was formed in my little heart that would stay with me for almost thirty years. The specifics are blurry but the impact is crystal clear. There was a season of time (I couldn't tell you how long it actually was) when my dad would come home from a long day of work with a little gift under his arm. A gift for me. It happened several times. Sometimes it would be Hot Wheels, sometimes Legos, other times a pack of Poopatroopers (still one of my favorites). It was completely unexpected at first. I'm not even sure why he bought them. My hunch is that these gifts were actually in some way more for my mom than they were for me, like an unwitting pawn in a peace meal to which I had no complaints. But it wouldn't take long for these gifts to move from the category of unexpected surprises to an expected contract of love. I wasn't sure why I was receiving them, but I was absolutely sure they would continue. Until the day when he came home empty-handed. I had Pavlovianly placed myself at the front door to see what would be under his arm that day and was confused as to why there was nothing. Maybe it was a gift so big that my dad couldn't bring it in by himself. I half hoped to see a couple of neighborhood dads helping unload it from his trunk, shaking their heads in the shame of being outdone. But there were no other dads in the driveway, the trunk was clearly closed, and his hands were obviously empty.

So I asked, "Dad, where's my gift?" "Gift?" he replied, as though this was the first time he had ever heard the word. "Yeah, my gift. What did you bring me today?" His answer was as empty as his arms. "Oh, sorry son, there's no gift today." No gift?! What does that mean? No gift? I thought for sure he was mistaken. And I gave him the benefit of the doubt and figured that he would make up for it the next day. But he did not. In fact, the next gift I received from him wouldn't come until Christmas—several disappointing months later. There had been a breach in contract, a break in our unspoken agreement. It was an innocent and disappointing moment that should have been lost in the shuffle of thousands of other innocent and disappointing moments. A moment I should have gotten over. But I didn't. I couldn't. What I didn't realize in that moment, what my dad couldn't realize in that moment, was that my little heart had already done the math. Somewhere in the back of all conscious thought, I reasoned that this is how it works. My dad was shaping my perception of God. I reasoned that God's love and goodness are at best random, at worst contingent on me holding up my side of some unspoken and unclear agreement. Much of my relationship with God would be built from the blueprint of this moment.

The early conception of God is almost invariably founded upon the child's idea of his father.

J. B. Phillips

Years later I would agree upon a good working relationship with God where I wouldn't ask for much from him, just that he keep the little gifts coming. I never prayed to win the lottery. I never prayed that God would bring my grandfather back from the dead. That would be too much. Instead I would settle for and come to depend on the daily little gifts of good health, minimal pain and loss, and to be well liked by others. Nothing extravagant, just the basics. In return I would follow him. I would be a good kid who did the things God wanted good kids to do. Nothing extravagant, just the basics. It was a good plan, one that worked for almost twenty years. But this plan wouldn't work forever, it couldn't. The reality of life would change this unspoken and unclear arrangement, and it wouldn't be long until the life I had built on the shallow foundation of this God came crashing down around me. It just stopped working. God no longer lived on these terms, which led me to wonder if he ever had at all, or if I had ever even actually known God at all. In the fallen rubble of a God built from my parents, I would begin to question not only what I had done with my life, but more important, what God had done with it ... or better put, *to* it.

The role a parent plays in shaping a child's view of God is palpable and unavoidable. How could it be anything else? Your parents are your first and most formidable window into affection, acceptance, strength, tenderness, authority, stability, and love. Their ability to give you what you need, as well as their inability to do so, all goes into the mix of who you perceive God to be and how you experience him well beyond your childhood. Good and bad. Right and wrong. Words and actions. Spoken and unspoken. In their presence and in their absence. Whether they realized it or not. Whether you realize it or not.

I'm amazed at how often it comes up as I listen to people's stories. Like my friend Lisa, whose dad has yet to say "I love you" to her. He has managed to make it twenty-two years by saying nothing more than "Me too" to his daughter's desire for verbal affirmations of love. She is now left with a distant God who is uninterested and unimpressed.

Or my friend J.D., who at eight years old circled in the Service Merchandise catalog a clock radio he desperately wanted, to which his mother told him to work hard and save up and he could buy it himself. He has been following a God that has asked nothing less of him than to take care of his business on his own. To make for himself the life God is unwilling to get involved in.

Or my friend Doug, who discovered after thirty years that his mom is more affectionate and affirming of their family cat than she ever was of any of her kids.

Or my friend Scott, whose dad left his mom and him when he was four years old. By his fifth birthday, he was given the gift of becoming the man of the house. One day when he was seven and out front playing basketball with a friend, his mom came home from work and he proceeded to tell her about a leak in the hall bathroom. Before she even got to the door, she demanded to know what kind of leak it was and why he hadn't called a plumber yet. To which his little soul screamed, "I'm seven!" He has followed a God who has demanded from him nothing less than everything, all the while dangling the twin carrots of rest and delight five feet from his work-worn face.

Then there's Jack, whose dad liked to take his fears and frustrations out in the form of a fist. This friend longed to experience the love of God in the absence of fear. He wanted to believe in a God who unconditionally loved him just as he was. But the possibility would prove to be too

5½ Glimpses of God
(Courtesy of My Parents)

1. The hand of justice

   As kids, my brother and I loved running upstairs and climbing into bed with my parents. As we snuggled up on each side of my dad, he would raise his hand and begin swaying it back and forth, ready to topple on one of us. We would flinch and giggle with each passing swoop until eventually it would fall right on the gut of one of us, only to start tickling. That swaying hand gave me a glimpse of a wild but loving God who utterly delights in his children.

2. A family that scares together

   In acts that would have the Department of Children and Family Services on high alert, my dad would hide behind doors and in closets waiting to scare whoever should be so unfortunate to cross his path. The best scare, the one that made me wet my Star Wars sheets, was when he hid under my bed and waited until I climbed in and got comfy. With an indiscernible growl, he reached up and grabbed me. This is why I can't wait to be a dad. That shock and laughter was a glimpse into the joy (and the fear) of God.

3. This is what it sounds like when dads cry

   One year on Mother's Day, I was waiting in front of the TV for my dad to get ready so we could go to church. Instead, he came out to the family room weeping. He confessed that he never got to tell his mom he loved her before she died. He begged me to make sure I tell my mom I love her every chance I get. Through his tears, he gave me a glimpse of the beautiful and broken heart of God.

4. Wrap it up

I was twenty years old and still living at my parents' house. In an attempt to teach me a lesson, my parents gathered up everything that lay on the floor of my fallout shelter of a room and put it in trash bags. They then took those bags and put them in the trunk of a friend's car and told me they had thrown them away. I got my stuff back after a week and moved out by the end of the year. They did unknowingly teach me another lesson—that God is a God of unpredictable consequences who can act without warning.

5. Let's talk about sex ... better yet, let's not

My parents never gave me "the talk." Actually, that's not entirely true. My mom did randomly turn to me while driving in the car once and blurt, "You know, oral sex and sex are no different!" And that was it. Although I had never had oral sex, or sex, for that matter, my mom gave me a glimpse of a God who has little to say about my sexuality other than "stop!" While we're on the topic of sex ...

5½. Let's give 'em something to talk about

When I was in college, my mom walked into my room right in the middle of a serious make-out session with the girl I was dating at the time. Needless to say, she didn't talk to me for a couple days. (And by "she" I mean my mom ... and my girlfriend.)

perplexing. At age twenty-seven, just three days after spending a lunch break with me, laughing, crying, and praying to the God he desperately wanted to believe in, he would take his own life.

If you had to describe the God you've found floating in the wake of your parents' presence in your life, what would this God look like? How have their best and worst attempts and intentions been used to shape the God you think you know? What was it? Was it a divorce? An affair? Maybe it was an emotionally absent parent. Or an over-demanding parent. A parent who in many ways was still a child themselves. A parent who gave you everything you wanted but very little of what you needed. A domineering parent. A parent who wielded shame and guilt like weapons of mass destruction. A parent who was incapable of showing physical affection. A parent who set unreachable expectations. An alcoholic parent. An abusive parent. The list could keep going.

This is big stuff. The stuff of good counseling and spiritual mentors. These are questions worth facing. Questions that are in no way an attempt to destroy or tear down your parents or mine, but I hope they lead to a healthy understanding of not only God, but also our parents.

I'll never forget driving in the car with my mom, coming back from the hospital where my dad was recovering from open-heart surgery. I asked her what she thought of my generation's fascination with digging in the dirt of our past. Her answer was completely in keeping with the culture she grew up in. "I don't see what good can come from it. I don't see what the point is of digging up the pain and problems of my past. How does it help me to point out all the things my father didn't do right? If you ask me, it's just another way of scapegoating the responsibility that each of us must bear for our own lives and our own choices." I

WHAT MARVELOUS LOVE THE FATHER HAS EXTENDED TO US! JUST LOOK AT IT—WE'RE CALLED CHILDREN OF GOD! THAT'S WHO WE REALLY ARE. BUT THAT'S ALSO WHY THE WORLD DOESN'T RECOGNIZE US OR TAKE US SERIOUSLY, BECAUSE IT HAS NO IDEA WHO HE IS OR WHAT HE'S UP TO.

1 JOHN 3:1 MSG

understand where she is coming from, and I couldn't disagree more. While it's true that many get stuck in the false liberation of finger-pointing and finding fault in everything their parents did, I believe there is more there, deeper, underneath the surface where the seeds of life take root and begin to grow.

I am not interested in deferring the debt of my own choices and responsibilities. I am in no way blaming my parents for my issues with God. This is not that. This is digging in the dirt of our own stories. This is accepting that your parents, despite their best and worst attempts, weren't perfect and have contributed to your perception of and experience with God more than almost anything else in your life. This is ultimately about putting to death any and all surrogate gods that have kept you from knowing and experiencing the true father/mother heart of God. That's what this is all about. That's what you and I have been given the gift and responsibility to do if we are ever to truly know God as Jesus did, as his Abba, his daddy, his perfect parent.

I pray in all faith and humility that you will begin to see God clearly through the fog of your parents' role and influence in your life. That he will emerge in truth and reveal to you his perfect, loving, fatherly and motherly heart. I pray this for you and for me. I pray this for my children, knowing full well they will one day need God to do the same work in their lives. To anyone who has ever had parents, this is my prayer and desire, that you would know God for who he is and who he is not, and that you will recognize him as the source of all that is beautiful in your parents and as the redeemer of all that is broken. This is your God ... and you are his child.

Show and Tell

I do not want my image of God, I want God.

C. S. Lewis

My friend Shane Claiborne has a great way of describing the "Christian life." He sums it all up by saying, "Jesus wrecks everything!" Contrary to the beliefs of many late-night blinged-out televangelists, Jesus really does wreck a lot of what we call life. He wrecks the comfy, cozy lives we build for ourselves. He messes up the neat little boxes we try to fit him into. He wrecks the subtle yet destructive images of God we've spent our whole lives building. Ultimately (and I hope), if we get close enough, Jesus wrecks us too.

While Jesus was on this earth, he completely wrecked the images and assumptions people had of God. For starters, Jesus talked about God in simply shocking ways. In a culture that took deep pride in its devout reverence for God (so much so that no one was even allowed to say the name of God out loud without having large and painful rocks chucked at them), Jesus preached about God as his *Abba*, which literally translates to the word "Daddy." Jesus talked about God as if he actually knew God. And no one quite knew how to respond. It's like being a kid and catching your parents in a passionate kiss. While it's great to know they do that, you really don't have a framework for that kind of in-your-face intimacy. Okay, maybe it's not totally like catching your parents making out, but you get the idea. Jesus came with what seemed like a completely new framework for God, even though God himself hadn't changed since humanity took its first breath from his lips. But somehow with Jesus, everything seemed different. Suddenly the outcasts and outsiders were drawn in and the religious rulers and power brokers felt marginalized and powerless. The lame learned to dance while the proud and stubborn stumbled away.

Jesus used everyday images — sheep, fields, pay-checks, grapevines, children, and neighbors — to reveal deep theological concepts about who God is and who we are. Just as God had breathed life into the dust pile of humanity thousands of years before, Jesus breathed life into everyday, overlooked, ordinary things. Suddenly everything was alive and somehow spiritual and somehow pointing to a God who was both bigger and closer than anyone could dare to imagine.

But Jesus did more than just tell us about God. Ultimately, Jesus wrecked everything by showing us who he was — the Son of God. Jesus spoke of himself in some pretty audacious ways. He had the nerve to claim he was God's Son. Then he took things a step further when he claimed not only to be God's Son, but to actually be God. Not a good idea if you're looking to get in with the religious elite or to establish a lifelong messianic career. It's the type of talk that gets a person killed. But Jesus knew exactly what he was doing. He was breaking through the myths and misconceptions that had clouded God for thousands of years. He was revealing God.

The Bible tells us that in Jesus we see the very image of God. So here was Jesus — the very image of God — painting startlingly fresh and soul-stirring images of God. Showing and telling. As Brennan Manning puts it,

"Everything we need to know about God we can find in the life of Jesus." If that's true, then it makes sense that if we want to have a clear image of God, we should, at the very least, look to Jesus.

Part 2

Constructive Images That Shape Us

Late-Night Neighbor

Late-Night Neighbor

I'm cheap. This is a well known and seldom cele-brated fact about me. I'm cheap and I don't like to share (a winning combination indeed). Go to the movies with me and you can expect to have to get your own pop-corn and Sour Patch Kids. My laptop, my iPod, my DJ gear, these are items that seldom leave my sight without implicit instructions and a little internal resistance. It's a trait that God takes great delight in refining in my life.

Like the time we let one of our interns move into our house until he could find a place of his own. What we didn't know was that the dude was fully herbal and popped no less than twenty-five vitamins a day. Within days our house reeked of Vitamin B. Or the time another intern asked if he could borrow my twelve-year-old, no-frills Chevy Cavalier for the weekend (a car generously given to me by my brother Scott). I thought to myself, *What Would Jesus Do?* While I was thinking about that, my mind began to wander. I thought to myself, *What would Jesus drive? It would probably be a sweet 1978 El Camino ...* Before I got lost in the image of Jesus drag racing, my mind snapped back. Jesus would let the kid borrow the car, unless maybe he knew (which I didn't) that the small detail this intern failed to include was that he needed the car so he could drive it to St. Louis! Or the time we let some good friends of ours crash at our place for a couple of weeks in between house closings before they moved into their new house. Crash they did, right into our brand new front porch as they backed their moving truck filled with all their earthly belongings into our driveway. Maybe this is why I'm so stingy with my stuff. Maybe this is why God gives me so many opportunities to loosen the death grip I have on my things. Maybe there is something about his heart that he has been trying to reveal.

I am thankful God is nothing like me. And in Luke 11, Jesus tells a story that gives us a glimpse not only into the utterly available heart of God, but into our hearts of boldness and reluctance. It's a story that confused its hearers just as much in Jesus' day as it does today. It goes something like this:

It's midnight at the oasis and everyone is in bed. The family is asleep in the upper floor of the house. Sleeping beneath them on the radiant dirt floor are the family's animals — some sheep, a few chickens, and even their donkey (who is prone to night terrors). This was how it worked in Jesus' day. Everything and everyone was kept in the house, and sleep came only after everything and everyone was quiet. On this particular night all was still . . . until a knock came at the door. The father wonders if it might be a burglar. If so, he was a very considerate burglar. Few burglars knock anymore. The knocks grow with intensity, interspersed with the occasional "pssst . . . pssst." The father rolls over in bed. He chooses to believe that it's all a dream — a loud, repetitive, annoying dream. The knocking continues to get louder until the father reluctantly crawls out of bed, grabs a baseball bat, and makes his way to the window. It's his neighbor, Al.

The father musters up the words "Go away!" in a raspy voice that registers somewhere between a whisper and a yell. The father climbs back in bed, hoping he's the only one who heard the midnight nuisance. It's too late. The sheep are the first to wake up, then the chickens, though the donkey somehow manages to stay asleep through it all. The knocks continue. Al clearly hasn't gone away. The father begrudgingly makes his way to the door. Across it is a heavy beam, there to keep intruders out ... a lot of good that's doing. The father opens the door to see Al standing there, wearing nothing more than his pajamas and a smile that apparently needs little sleep.

Al proceeds to break into a story about his in-laws who have been planning a trip for months and who, unbeknownst to Al, just pulled up in their RV out front. As the father strains to figure out what all this has to do with him, Al cuts to the chase. "The wife and I don't have anything to feed them ... So, what I was wondering, neighbor, was ... can I borrow a couple of loaves of bread?" *Bread? You want to borrow bread? Do you have any idea what time it is?* The father, half hoping he had opened the door to a burglar, stands there staring in amazement at Al, whose only response is a shrug of the shoulders that says, "Whadya gonna do?" The father is half tempted to slam the door in Al's face and go back to bed, but he can't. He can see the lights on next door; he can hear Al's mother-in-law laughing, a noise that pierces the soft serenity of midnight. The father knows what he has to do. He knows that if he says no, the other neighbors will hear about it. He knows that Al wouldn't have knocked if he didn't really need the bread, and more importantly, he knows that Al never would have knocked if he didn't wholeheartedly believe the father would give it to him. The father goes to the kitchen, grabs the bread that he was looking forward to eating in the morning, and gives it to Al. His motivation comes not from the goodness and generosity of his heart, but out of the sheer shock and hidden delight in a neighbor who would ask so boldly. Al gladly receives the bread, and before the father can ask when he's going to return his lawnmower, Al is gone, shouting over his shoulder, "Thanks neighbor, I owe you one." *Try three!*

The gift of this story comes, like all of Jesus' stories, wrapped in the glossy paper of context. The story does not stand alone. Nor does this perplexing image of God. First of all, this image comes at the end of a very important moment for Jesus and his disciples. After years of watching and listening to Jesus pray, his disciples finally get up the nerve to ask him how they can pray like he does. What Jesus told them was, "When you pray, say, 'Father, hallowed be your name, your kingdom come. Give us each day our daily bread. Forgive us our sins, for we also forgive everyone who sins against us. And lead us not into temptation' " (Matthew 6).

Perhaps the most famous prayer of all, it is known as the Lord's Prayer, or my personal favorite, the "Our Father." It is the basis of the intimate moments Jesus spent with his Abba. If this prayer Jesus prays is a glimpse of what to say, then this story Jesus tells is a glimpse of what to expect. Give us this day our daily bread ... even if it comes at midnight. Jesus is painting multiple layers of comparison. Comparisons that are fully fleshed out in an epilogue to this particular story.

Jesus, sensing that his disciples weren't quite getting it all, cuts to the chase in Luke 11:9–10:

"So I say to you: Ask and it will be given to you;
seek and you will find; knock and the door will be
opened to you. For everyone who asks receives;
those who seek find; and to those who knock,
the door will be opened."

Jesus pauses. His disciples' eyes are still squinting, the corners of their mouths now revealing the drool of dumbfoundedness. Jesus looks past them to the crowd now listening in.

"Which of you fathers, if your son asks for a fish,
will give him a snake instead? Or if he asks for an egg,
will give him a scorpion? If you then, though you are evil,
know how to give good gifts to your children,
how much more will your Father in heaven give
the Holy Spirit to those who ask him!"

Luke 11:11–13

Jesus is playing to our basic human decency, our good neighborly selves that would, if put in a similar situation, respond similarly to the father in Jesus' story. His assumption is that most of us (certainly not all) would help an elderly woman carry the groceries to her car. Or that most of us (certainly not all) would stop to help a broken down motorist change a flat on the side of the road. It's what good citizens do, what good neighbors do, what good fathers do. Certainly you, at some point in your life, have depended on the kindness of strangers or have been that stranger for someone else. It is on this foundation that Jesus builds this image of God.

"If," Jesus proposes, "you would help a stranger change a flat, how much more will your Father in heaven help you? If you would loan your neighbor your Weedwacker, how much more do you think your father wants to give you all that you need?" Again evoking the image of a good father, he says to all the parents in the house, "If your kid asks for Kool-Aid, who in their right mind would fill their sippy cup with paint thinner?" It's a no-brainer to Jesus. If we, as selfish, fallen, and flawed people, would help our kids and neighbors, how much more will our Father in heaven take care of us? The question is never one of whether or not God will provide, but rather, will you ask him to?

"Ask and ye shall receive, seek and ye shall find, knock and it shall be opened unto you"—what are these famous words but an invitation to reach out for the Permanent and the Real? If we want to co-operate, the Spirit is immediately available.

J. B. Phillips

This may be perhaps one of the greatest tragedies of what we have come to call Christianity: that we are all too afraid to ask a good and loving God for what he already longs to give us. We have been raised in a culture that has approached prayer with a sense of reverence and reservation that can sometimes border on fear and timidity. Prayers smothered in the repetitive reluctance of such phrases as "If it be your will," "If it pleases you," "If you can." Prayers that prefer, in place of knocking, to leave a polite note slid under the door at the gates of heaven.

Don't get me wrong, I know that God has a thing for holy fear, and we should too. But God also has a thing for confident assuredness, an assurance afforded us by the death and resurrection of Jesus Christ. An assurance ever available as revealed in Hebrews 4:16: "Let us then approach God's throne of grace with confidence, so that we may receive mercy and find grace to help us in our time of need."

A Primer on Freeloading

Ten phrases you should be familiar with when dealing with your freeloading friends. To properly assess your friends, place a check next to any of the phrases that your friends have used with you in the last year.

✓ "Are you gonna eat that?"
✓ "You know, refills are free here ... so ... are you done with your cup?"
✓ "You own a truck, right?"
✓ "What are you doing on the last Saturday of this month?" (Numbers 3 and 4 are typically used in tandem.)
✓ "I don't actually have a student ID with me, but I consider myself a student of life."
✓ "Dude, do you mind giving me a ride to the DMV? It will only take a minute."
✓ "It's nothing permanent, I just need a place to crash for the next couple of ~~days, weeks~~, months."
✓ "Do you mind getting this one? I'll get the next."

✓ "Is it cool if I borrow your iPod for my trans-European backpack trip?"

✓ "Yes, I did borrow your jacket ... No, I didn't *personally* smoke while wearing it ... and as far as I know, you can get blood out of almost anything these days."

Now it's time to ~~judge~~ rate your friends. Add up your score and see below:

0–3—You've got great friends whom you can trust with your stuff. Feel free to loan them your Weedwacker this weekend.

4–7—You've got some good friends, but odds are your Weedwacker is already in one of their garages.

8–10—These folks are not your friends. They are pirates parading as nice people. They no longer have the Weedwacker you loaned them last weekend ... they just sold it on eBay.

Why then, Jesus asks the crowd gathered around him (and you gathered around these words), would you ever hesitate to ask God to do what he has already promised he would? It would seem, based on Jesus' teaching and the reality of our lives and prayers, that the issue lies not with the one who waits to answer, but with the one who hesitates to ask.

A few summers back, my wife and I, along with a couple of friends, took a two-week trip to Zambia, Africa, to see what we could do to bring help, healing, and dignity to those suffering from AIDS. For anyone who has ever held death in their arms, you know that everything you thought you knew about God is utterly up for grabs. How could God allow this? Why wouldn't he stop this? Where is he in all this death? As we held orphan after orphan, my heart quietly began heading down the desolate path of doubt and disappointment with God. A path I might have become lost on, were it not for the words I heard prayed by the widowed women we were with.

It was in the alleyways of Chifubu that we were dragged to the front door of heaven. The women we met there were unlike anyone I had ever met in the States. These women prayed like lions! These women who had lost husbands, daughters, sisters, and sons prayed to a God they still believed in. They prayed to a God they depended on. There wasn't a whisper of the word "if," but rather every prayerful plea began with the word "because." "God, because of what you said ... God because of what you've done ... God because of who you are." Their prayers came from an unshakable, unbreakable place where death and AIDS and poverty were not welcome. What moved us most was not that they believed in God; I know many people who believe in God, this was not that. No, these women actually *believed* God. They believed that he was there, that he had not forgotten or forsaken them, and that he would give them exactly what they needed, if only they would ask. And ask they did. Begged and pleaded they did, that God would not only hear their prayers, not only keep his promises, not only give them what they desperately needed, but that he would be who he says he is. Loving, generous, slow to anger, abounding in love. These women did not ask, they expected. And what we saw on that day was not only the depth of God's heart, but the fear-filled emptiness of our own.

To know this God is to know that he is good. He is incomprehensibly good. Good beyond reason. Good beyond measure. Good beyond words. Good beyond what we deserve. And yet maybe, for you, embracing the goodness of God proves to be more difficult than accepting the reality of the very existence of God. You may be agnostic in a sense when it comes to believing (and ultimately trusting) in the goodness of God. You believe there is a God but are just unconvinced that he is truly good. Pain, struggle, disappointment, and the like may have coaxed you into believing God is out there, but he is too inconsistent, uncontrollable, or indifferent to be trusted. He is nothing more than a cosmic slot machine (a destructive image explored earlier in this book).

The image of God as a neighbor at midnight reveals as much about us as it is does about God. Here is a God who is good. Who longs to give us what we are so often afraid to ask for. A God who may not always give us what we want, but who will always give us what we need. He is a God who knows the needs of the orphan, the widow, the poor, the oppressed, the wealthy, the comfortable, the desperate, and the pseudo-secure. And he invites us to simply ask. He invites us to boldly ask. Never a whisper of the word "if," but every thought underlined with the word "because." Because of who he is. Because of his great love. Because of what he has done. Because of what he promised he will do. Because of what the Bible tells us to be true. Because of all of this, you can come ... even at midnight ... and ask.

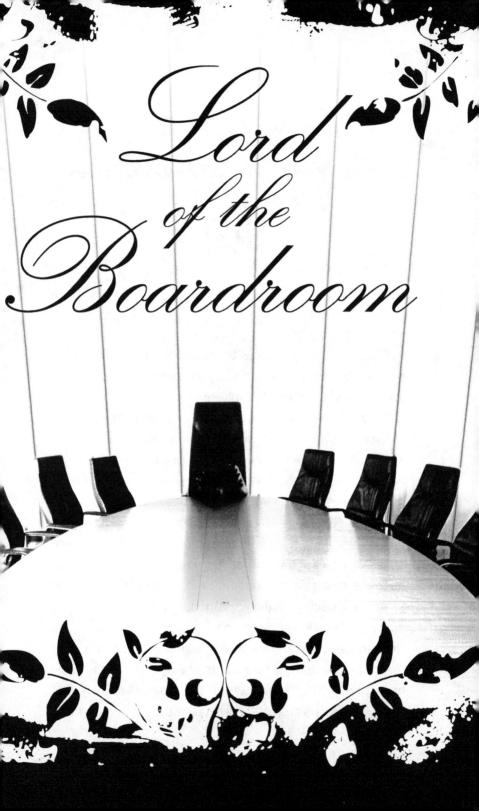

Lord of the Boardroom

I open this chapter with a small confession. It may not be the best way to start a chapter, but here we go (deep breaths ... inhale pink, exhale blue ...): My name is Jarrett Stevens and I'm a reality-TV addict. There, I said it. Even as I write these words, my television is inundated with reality-TV programming. I can't escape it—and to be honest, I'm not really sure I want to. I couldn't tell you what compels me to watch. It's like driving by a car accident; you know you shouldn't look, but you just can't help it. Maybe it has something to do with television's absurd concept of "reality." There's just something so *real* about a group of absolute strangers stranded on a deserted island, forced to speak Queen's English and undergo elective cosmetic surgery, while viewers vote on which contestant has to eat the carcass of an endangered species and which one has to propose marriage to a complete stranger. I can only hope that by the time you read this, the black plague of reality TV has passed and I am fully restored to my normal life.

Just for the record, I don't watch *every* reality show, only the "good" ones. One of my all-time favorites has to be Donald Trump's *The Apprentice* (back before it got lame!). Within its first season, it became an undisputed television phenomenon. Trump was suddenly cool again (that is, of course, assuming he was cool at some other point in human history). The concept of the show is fascinating. As far as I'm concerned, it should count as college credit for a business course, or better yet, a deviant psychology course. As someone who's done church work for a while now (and someone who's been a human for most of my life), I find the social dynamics, the glimpses of leadership, and the relentless fighting and backstabbing hopelessly addicting.

You probably know how the show works. Sixteen contestants compete in various challenges for the chance to win a high-paying job at one of Trump's companies. Contestants are divided into two teams that fight it out for most of each hour-long episode. The winners get some great reward (usually something that includes Trump's name). The losers, however, go through the humiliating ritual of packing up their stuff and wheeling their suitcases into the boardroom to face Donald Trump. This is the best part of the show. Trump and his two sidekicks ruthlessly grill each team member about why they failed and who on the team is the source of the problem. After ten minutes of grandstanding, self-promoting, and arguing, the contestants get their chance to speak. Then Trump typically gets fed up and makes his final decision. He looks across the boardroom table and snarls his now trademarked (yes, trademarked) words, "You're fired!" The contestants' reactions are worth the whole show. Some stare in silent shock. Some cry. Some storm out. Some try in vain to argue their case after the fact, which only makes Trump angrier. Regardless of the responses, the bottom line remains: "You're fired!" Cue cheesy dramatic music. Cue slow-motion shots of the contestants who didn't get fired walking back to the suite. Cue the loser riding off in a cab. Cue credits. Cue my TiVo for next week.

What is it about *The Apprentice* that made it the most-watched show in its debut season? What motivated an unprecedented number of people to wait hours and hours in casting call lines, and spend their precious time and money creating audition tapes, all with the hope of being selected as one of the show's sixteen contestants? What made one million people apply for the show's second season? One of those one million people being my wife, who made one of the best audition tapes I'd ever seen, where she coined the phrase, "My profit is people." Trump doesn't know what he missed out on. And while we're talking about "The Donald," would someone please help me understand how this guy can have all the fame, power, money, and influence he has and yet still sport an "onion-roll comb-over" hairdo? *Seriously.* My dad tried that look in the seventies and one million people didn't get in line to meet him.

Why are we so interested? Why do so many people (me being one of them) keep on watching? I think it has something to do with our unquenchable obsession with wealth and power. For sixty minutes a week, we get to dream about what we would do with all that money and power or what we might say to our boss if we ever had the guts. Wealth and power are age-old obsessions. Obsessions that have historically been misguided and greatly misused. Cue Jesus.

Jesus has an uncanny way of speaking right into our misguided obsessions and misinformed assumptions, and he often does it through the most unexpected means. A great example of this can be found in Luke 19:11–28.

It is a few short days before Jesus is crucified, and just hours before he makes his triumphal entry into Jerusalem. Here we have a glimpse of Jesus at one of the most critical junctures of his life and ministry. And where do we find him? According to Luke, he's leaving a party thrown in his honor by Zacchaeus, a recently reformed tax collector, a newly converted follower of Jesus.

As Jesus leaves the party and sets his steps toward the cross, he tells an odd little story. An often misunderstood yet thoroughly revealing story about the heart of God. Jesus spoke of a rich man who is called out of town to accept the title of "king" in a far-off land (think "Arnold Schwarzenegger, honorary degree"). This rich man takes his honorary kingship quite seriously, and so he carefully prepares for his long journey. Before leaving, he calls together his servants, gives each of them ten pounds of silver, and tells them to invest it for him while he is gone. And with that, the rich man leaves to go and pick up his new crown. But all is not well back home. Apparently, this rich man doesn't have a huge fan base, because shortly after returning home (his crown still in his carry-on) the people from his hometown rebel and refuse to recognize him as their king. They want a recount. Public approval ratings plunge, but that doesn't slow him down one bit. He calls his servants back together and asks each one to give an earnings report.

The first servant gives a great report—he doubled the amount he was given. The king is pleased and rewards the servant by letting him keep his earnings and appointing him governor of ten cities! Not a bad gig for someone who had been scrubbing the vomitorium just a month prior. The next servant also has a good report—he made a 50 percent profit. The king is again very pleased and rewards the man by letting him keep his earnings and appointing him governor of five cities! It's turning out to be a very good day in the kingdom ... until the king comes to the next servant. We'll call him Thrifty McSitsonarse. Driven by fear of failure and the shifting tides of public opinion, he chose to do nothing with the money he was given. Literally nothing. He could have locked it up in a nice, ninety-day CD, but he didn't. He could have opened up a first-time savings account at the corner bank and received a cute little puppy dog checkbook and a free set of steak knives. But he didn't. He did nothing. And his lame excuse? Speaking of his money to the king, the servant says, "I hid it and kept it safe. I was afraid because you are a hard man to deal with, taking what isn't yours and harvesting crops you didn't plant" (Luke 19:20–21 NLT).

Now, I've never actually spoken to a king before (other than a guy who came to my preschool dressed as Burger King to hand out balloons and free cheeseburgers), but my hunch is, when in the presence of a king, it's wise to keep one's words to a minimum. And when one does speak, one probably should not mock the king in front of everybody. One probably shouldn't call the king a fraud and a thief. But that's exactly what this third servant does! And he pays for it—royally. The king tears into him (Trump doesn't hold a candle to this king). He takes the ten pounds of silver the servant sat on and gives it to the first servant (thus bringing his grand total to 110 pounds of silver!). At this point in the story, Jesus states an often misunderstood and misused truth: "To those who use well what they are given, even more will be given. But from those who are unfaithful, even what little they have will be taken away" (Luke 19:26 NLT).

There's a lot to chew on here, but the story isn't over. The king turns his attention away from the wicked servant to the disgruntled mob that had gathered outside the palace doors. A protest of sorts had formed and the natives were getting restless. They refused to recognize him as king and demanded he be immediately removed from the throne. The king responds by ordering that everyone involved in this insurgence be brought into the throne room for a "special meeting." As soon as all are gathered, the king orders that every last one be executed for insubordination. He has them all killed right there in his courtroom, in front of everyone!

Imagine what the wicked servant must have felt. No doubt he assumed he was next. If the king could wipe out a bunch of angry protestors with a word, imagine what he might do to this servant. The tension in this story is piling up quicker than bodies on the palace floor, but strangely enough, this is where Jesus chooses to say, "The end." That's it. No resolve through revenge. No climactic confrontation. Because, according to Jesus, that's not really the point of the story. In fact, the point was already made and missed back at the beginning. So with a nod of the head and a glance from his soul-piercing eyes, Jesus walks on ahead of the crowd that had been walking with him, leaving them behind to sift through the confusing rubble of this story.

Instead of giving a cookie-cutter, fill-in-the-blank lesson about God, Jesus tells a story that is as compelling as it is confusing. The obscurity is intentional. We don't know why the rich man was called to another land to be named king. We don't know why the people from his town sent a delegation after him to protest his kingship. We just know the people in his hometown hated him. My hunch is that if these people were to dig a little deeper, they probably couldn't even articulate why they hated the man so much. Perhaps their contempt was based on their own shallow assumptions about power, or nasty rumors they had heard about this king. Or maybe it was just good old-fashioned envy. Maybe Jesus deliberately left things a little vague to give us room to fill in the blanks with some of our own unspoken assumptions about power and authority.

---

*It was pride and self-righteousness and
the exploitation of others
which called forth His greatest anger.*

J. B. Phillips

The blanks shouldn't be that hard to fill. We quickly jump to all our assumptions and stereotypes when we hear any bad news about CEOs of big companies. We do the same with elected officials whose opinions differ from our own. We do the same with the people who live in that huge house on the hill behind the gates. We do it with celebrities who seem to have everything we think we want. I do it with Oprah. I've never met Oprah but I convince myself I know everything about her—like her book club, to the money she's made, to Steadman. Here is a woman who has done more for African Americans, specifically African-American women, than almost anyone in recent history. A woman who has done more for the AIDS pandemic in Africa than all other talk show hosts combined. A woman who gave a guy like Dr. Phil a career. And yet, in my mind, because of her wealth, power, and celebrity, she's suspect. She's incapable of being "one of us." I feel like I know everything about her ... even though I've never even met her.

As easy as it is to fill in the blanks with our assumptions about people, it's even easier to do so with God. Because of God's power, because of God's "otherness," and because God exists in equal parts mystery and truth, it's easy to assume God is forever separate from us or,

It's so easy to fill in the blanks about other people without knowing the full story. Take a look at the following scenarios and see how quickly your mind jumps to stereotypes and assumptions.

- A really, really old and wealthy man marries a young, beautiful, silicon-enhanced woman.
- A telemarketer calls with an exciting "new opportunity" for you.
- A celebrity checks himself into a hospital (again) for undisclosed reasons.
- A local church pastor pulls up on Sunday morning in a shiny new BMW.
- The government raises the terror alert to fuchsia (or whatever the latest color is) right before an election.
- A hurricane hits the poor side of town and everyone is surprised.
- A guy who slept through most of the semester mysteriously gets an *A* on the final.
- Someone pulls up next to you at a stoplight in a Hummer with all the bells and whistles.
- Someone sees a Michael Moore film.

perhaps, even against us. It's easy to assume we can never truly know God, and therefore, God will never truly know us. Perhaps our assumptions about God and our responses to him are more like that of the wicked servant than we even realize.

In light of his fears and assumptions about the king, the wicked servant determined that the best course of action was to do absolutely nothing. The logic may seem a little backward at first, but it makes perfect sense to someone ruled by fear and misguided assumptions. It goes something like this: "Based on what I think I know about the king—that he is cruel, cold, and calculating—the best way for me to avoid failing him or disappointing him is to do absolutely nothing. If I don't try, I can't fail." This is the aim-low approach to life. And in this story (as it so often does in our stories) the do-nothing plan completely backfires and leaves the servant worse off than when he began.

So just what exactly is the moral of this story? Based on your initial thoughts (assuming that you haven't read ahead), what point do you think Jesus is trying to make?

The moral of the story seems pretty obvious at first glance: God rewards those who make something of themselves and punishes those who don't. Or, to put it more simply, "God helps those who help themselves." The only way to earn God's love and acceptance is to do just that—earn it! Even as I write these words about God, I am aware they could become nothing more than chips at the bargaining table of God's love for me. The more this book helps people, the more God will be pleased with me. The more God is pleased with me, the easier my life will be. But if this book stinks and the only people who buy it are my mom and my wife, where does that leave me? What good am I to God if I'm not doing something good for God? After all, isn't that what God really wants? Isn't that the moral of the story?

Fortunately, Jesus makes an entirely different point than we might expect. Look again at what the king in the story does with all his profits. Does he say anything about fattening the national treasury or reinvesting the profits in a high-yield, low-risk money market account? No, the king gives all of the initial seed money and all of the profits to his servants. Not only that, he gives away fifteen cities in his new kingdom. In the end, this cruel, cold, and calculating king gives away over 160 pounds of his silver and fifteen of his cities.

Here is an utterly mind-boggling and potentially soul-stirring concept of God that has perplexed humanity since we took our first breaths: God is both just *and* generous. God can both keep us to our end of the deal and forgive us when we fall short. God holds in one hand the power to wipe out an angry mob, and in the other hand the power to give away the keys to the kingdom.

How long have I imagined God as a fearful CEO rather than the loving Father Jesus describes? How often have I missed the goodness and generosity of God because of my distance and preconceived assumptions? Clues to God's great generosity abound. They surround my life in seen and unseen ways. And yet somehow, I so often miss them. By way of reminder (for me as much as for you), here are just a few glimpses of God's great generosity.

There is the gift of my wife Jeanne, whom I know better than anyone and yet whose depth and love still surprise me each day. There is the moon at 1:00 a.m., bright and proud and my quiet company on sleepless nights. There is my dog Molly, whose love would be completely unconditional were it not for her relentless expectation that I play tug-of-war with every branch she finds. There are things like sex and sleep and food (not always in that order), all of which could be numbingly utilitarian, but God in his generosity created them to be deeply pleasurable. In a world where there is the undeniable presence of AIDS, death, heartbreak, pain, and longing, there is also love, laughter, forgiveness, and friends who light up when they see you. And while I wrestle with understanding God's role in the former, I should not be confused about God's presence in the latter. This is the moral of our story, that in a world filled with pain and fear and confusion, there is a God who is more good, more generous, and more full of grace than we could possibly imagine. And as wildly as he offers himself to us, so should we offer ourselves to him, no longer living in the risk-free distance of all our assumptions, but up close and personal, so we can see just how good and generous this King truly is.

Green-thumbed Gardener

Green-Thumbed Gardener

*M*y foray into lawn care was nothing short of a disaster. I was thirteen and my family had just moved into a new house in a brand new housing development. The house was great, with a beautiful view of the San Francisco Bay. Everything about the house was new, except for the backyard. The enormous backyard must have been the contractor's last item on an apparently abandoned to-do list. In between our beautiful new house and our beautiful new view, lay a quarter-acre of desolate desert. It was nothing but dirt and weeds. And not just any weeds, these were angry weeds that defied anyone who dared touch them. Their roots were thick and deep, their branches filled with thorns and thistles. Round about the time I began to feel sorry for the poor landscaper who would have to face this challenge, my dad informed me that I would be the one the family was sending into that wilderness wasteland we called a backyard.

I spent days in that yard attempting to remove three-foot-tall weeds that had been waiting for me their entire lives. It was hard work. Those weeds were willful and the soil was utterly uncooperative. Everyone knows the proper way to remove a weed is to pull it up by its roots. It's unquestionably the right way to do it; it's just not the fastest. After checking into the availability of commercial napalm, and running a few "scorched earth" scenarios, I decided that the only way I was ever going to finish was to compromise my high work standard and begin breaking the weeds off at the ground. I was shocked and pleased at how much faster it went and how it looked like I had actually done the work. My revised plan worked beautifully . . . for about a week. It was then that the insurgence of weeds returned—reborn, reinvigorated, and fighting mad. I would spend the rest of the summer engaging in hand-to-hand combat with the weeds on their turf and on their terms. It only took one summer for me to learn just how much I hate gardening.

But my adventures in gardening were far from over. After buying our first house, I was informed by my wife Jeanne about my new role as the unpaid groundskeeper of our family. It was a role I relished at first. Mowing, edging, trimming, weeding when necessary. I was coming to peace with the earth. But that peace would be short-lived and soon replaced with a deep-rooted envy in my heart. I was proud of my little yard, until I looked over the fence and noticed my neighbor's yard—so clean, so creative, so much better than mine. Everywhere I went I saw yards that put mine to shame. Meticulously manicured and lovingly landscaped yards that made it clear to me that the grass actually is greener on the other side of the fence, so long as you know what fertilizers to use and when. In an attempt to keep my yard not only looking good, but better than everyone else's, I resorted to cupboards full of chemicals, sprays, and special tools used at just the right time. It's a never-ending battle that only further enforces what I knew during that wilderness wasteland of my youth—the secret to a good garden is a great gardener.

Ever the contextualist, Jesus pulls from the soil of our story an image that everyone could understand. He speaks of gardening. An image that casts himself as the vine, us as the branches, and his Father as the gardener. The power of the image must be explored if we are to understand and trust our green-thumbed gardener God. After all, it was in a garden that it all began, where humanity was hand-planted by God and rose from the fresh soil of creation. It is there in the garden that God tended to Adam and Eve, not only nurturing them with his love, but inviting them into the metaphor as they cared for the garden themselves. God caring for them, them caring for the garden. This is where the image begins, this is what Jesus is taking us back to.

It was with the motive and attitude of the heart, i.e. the emotional center, that [Christ] was concerned. It was this that He called on men to change, for it is plain that once the inner affections are aligned with God, the outward expression of the life will look after itself.

J. B. Phillips

In John 15, in the final moments of relative peace before his crucifixion, in his final words with his followers before they would abandon him, Jesus continues to reveal the heart of the Father. He has told them what is to come, he has prepared them for life in the absence of the immediate physical presence of Jesus. But they are scared. So Jesus gives them these words: "I am the true vine, and my Father is the gardener" (John 15:1).

Jesus uses the image of a vine, most likely a grape-vine typical to the ones found in Middle Eastern vineyards. Unlike the beautiful roaming vineyards of the Napa Valley, vineyards in Jesus' day were smaller and lower to the ground. Vines did not grow up, but out, atop the soil. They were planted far enough apart so the gardener could walk in between them, inspecting them, correcting them, and after three years of being planted, harvesting them. All of it was done by hand. The soil tested and prepared, the seeds planted and watered, the branches properly placed and pruned for maximum growth.

Jesus is not speaking here of the macro-managed crop fields of "fly-over" states. The ones we see out airplane windows. Those perfect circles and squares of acres and acres of wheat and corn. Crops that are planted and harvested not by hand, but by machines. Giant John Deeres plowing through as crop dusters perform perfectly executed fly-bys. Out of necessity we have perfected the art of harvesting to a science of large-scale proportions. Human contact all but diminished. A far cry from my little backyard masterpieces. A far cry from the dirty fingernails and hands of God. Hands that plant and water and weed and prune. Hands that are intimately familiar and unafraid of the dirty soil of this world. Hands that reach in deep, that hold up straight, that carefully inspect, that provide for every need. God cannot garden from a distance. It is in the trusting intimacy of the presence of God that we can grow.

When the disciples want nothing more than answers to their questions of what to do next, Jesus shows them who they are, or rather, where they are in relation to the Father and the Son. Before we can begin to understand what we are to do with our lives, we must know who the Father is and who is his Son. He answers their questions by revealing

A Gardening Shortcut

Let's face it: gardening is hard! What, with all the dirt and watering and being out in the sun and planting and pruning, it's a wonder anyone does it at all. That's why the good folks at Joseph Enterprises gave us one of the greatest gifts the gardening world has ever seen: the Chia Pet. That's right, the Chia Pet. It doesn't get any easier than that. The only thing on this planet easier to grow than a Chia Pet is mold (believe me, I know).

So if you're in the mood for some small sprouting fun, grab a Chia Pet and make sure to follow these simple instructions, and you, too, will be growing beautiful Chia Pets in no time flat. (Note: the makers of Chia Pet make no guarantees that you will grow things in no time flat. In most cases it takes 4–5 days to properly grow a Chia Pet, and even then it doesn't look anything like the ones on the commercial.)

Step One: Take your Chia Pet out of the box.

Step Two: Ask yourself why you ever bought a Chia Pet in the first place.

Step Three: Fill your Chia Pet with water.

Step Four: Rub the packet of seeds all over the Chia Pet with a knife, preferably not the one you're using to cut your sandwich.

Step Five: Wait until something happens (hopefully growth of some sort).

Step Six: Watch something happen (hopefully growth of some sort).

Step Seven: Revel in the divine beauty that is the Chia Pet. And feel a small sense of satisfaction knowing that you are doing your part to keep this world green (never mind the fact that 437 Chias died to make the box that your Chia Pet came in ... the box you forgot to recycle).

not only who the Father is, but what the Father does: "He cuts off every branch in me that bears no fruit, while every branch that does bear fruit he prunes so that it will be even more fruitful" (John 15:2).

This then is what the Good Gardener does—watching and working, cutting and pruning. The image, while slightly foreign, is not an easy one. Cutting and pruning involves pain and blades and loss, none of which get anyone excited. Pruning is a critically misunderstood aspect of gardening. It involves cutting back or cutting off any branches that are fruitless or dead on the vine. It seems kind of cruel or careless, but it is essential. Without pruning, fruitless branches will continue to draw the water and nutrients that the rest of the plant needs. In essence, these "dead" branches starve the rest of the plant, taking life and giving back nothing in return.

That's all fine and good—God is a gardener, he prunes. Great. Lovely concept. But what does that have to do with us? What are we supposed to do?

> "Remain in me, as I also remain in you.
> No branch can bear fruit by itself; it must
> remain in the vine. Neither can you bear fruit
> unless you remain in me."

John 15:4

His command couldn't be any simpler. Jesus is telling his disciples to do what he has always told them to do. They are to stay connected to the life vine of Jesus. Stay. The hills we must take, the battles we must fight, the commissions we must fulfill, are always superseded by the simple act of staying. Before you go, you stay. Before you grow, you stay. The Vine knows exactly what it must do. The Gardener knows exactly what he must do. All the branch needs to do is stay. It is when we stay that we know.

"Be still, and know that I am God."

Psalm 46:10

It is when we stay that we grow.

"I am the vine; you are the branches.
If you remain in me and I in you, you will bear much fruit;
apart from me you can do nothing."

John 15:5

Our job couldn't be any simpler: All we have to do is stay. It's amazing how I struggle and strive and stray when all I've ever been asked to do is stay. The promise is clear—stay with me, connect to me, drawing your life from me, and you will not only grow, but you will bear fruit. You are supposed to bear fruit. You were created to grow and bear fruit. You have something of worth and wonder to give to this world. You are not supposed to be the same yesterday, today, and tomorrow—that's God's job. Your job is to grow and give of yourself the life that has been given to you. Jesus goes on in John 15:8 to say that it is by your fruit that the world will know who you belong to. In other words, not only were you created to grow, but you were created to bear much fruit. Not only were you created to bear much fruit, but your fruit is to be a gift to the world that points back to the work of the gardener in your life.

But there is also a warning in Jesus' words. It is as clear as the promise. Stray from me, and you will find your life empty, disconnected, and ultimately fruitless. You cannot and will not grow on your own. It is only by the hand of the gardener, connected to the vine of Jesus, within the safety of the garden, that you will grow. To expect otherwise is to be disappointed and disconnected from the life you were created to live.

Connectedness starves our selfishness. Our self-will and determination will always believe that we are better on our own, away from the confines of the garden, free from the hand of the gardener. Our self-centeredness will always convince us that it is all about us. Instead of offering the fruit of our lives to the world, we will take whatever we think we need from whomever we think we can get it. Left to ourselves, we will break off from the vine, inch away from the gardener, and go outside the garden ... where we will die.

Round about the time I thought I knew what I was doing in my yard, I had to go and introduce a foreign element—our ever inquisitive and perpetually peeing yellow Labrador, Molly. Molly is not a respecter of gardens. As a puppy she had a taste for the finer things, namely our beautifully crafted hydrangeas. She went after them like cotton candy at the county fair. Eating and digging until her work was done. And that's to say nothing for what she's done to the lawn. She is an artist of sorts, adding splashes of yellow burnt out grass to an otherwise green lawn. I tried to create a space for her to take care of her business. I hauled two tons of river rock from the Home Depot to a spot behind our garage. It was a beautiful space, created just for her to do what she felt she had to do. But she would have none of it. She fancied our soft and supple grass as the place she would leave her mark. After our first summer with Molly we were left with abstract patches of green and yellow, death and life. Even now I continue to do battle with her bladder. As soon as I'm finished with this chapter, I'm going out to mow what's left of our yard. I have spent the better part of this summer raking, fertilizing, planting, watering, replanting, and eventually sodding over the damage she has done. We have even resorted to giving her doggy supplements (creatively named "Green-ums") that actually change her pH balance and remove the acidity from her pee. We've just about done it all. All this caring for my grass has proven to be an endless effort that has yielded little more than a war-torn battlefield where green grass once grew. It seems as though my work in the yard is never done.

How true this is of our Gardener God, whose work is never done. Just when things begin to grow and bring life, disease enters in, weeds sprout up, rain doesn't come, and to top it all off, a dog comes along and pees all over us. His work is never done, not only because of the elements of the environment we live in, but also because (if not chiefly because) we refuse to stay still. We refuse to grow. We refuse to remain. We refuse to trust the gardener.

Contrary to popular belief and unspoken suspicion, we do not find God as the puppet master we might have imagined—manipulating, controlling, void of freedom, life, and will. Instead, Jesus introduces us to a God who walks through the garden of this world lovingly cultivating and crafting a space for us to do what we were created to do—to grow. This gardener knows and cares for every branch. He never stops. He knows when and where to water, to weed, to prune. He is the one who does the work. A branch cannot see the whole of the garden. A branch cannot control a single one of the elements. A branch cannot will its way to grow. A branch cannot survive on its own. It lives and grows and bears fruit only by the hand of the gardener.

Why then are we so intent on taking care of ourselves? Why do we work so hard to create and protect a life for ourselves on our own terms and by our own efforts? Why are we so preoccupied with seeing a mighty forest through the little branches of our lives? Why do we feel like we have so little to offer this world? Why do words like love, joy, peace, patience, kindness, goodness, faithfulness, gentleness, and self-control seem more like good ideas, than actual realities that flow from our lives? Why do we find it so hard to trust the one who planted us and knows us, and who longs for us to grow? Why won't we just stay?

Could it be that we have missed the God of green thumbs? The God that Jesus trusted to guide, to guard, and to shape his every decision, his every relationship, his every day, his very life? Could it be that all your striving and struggling to craft and create a life for yourself in the shallow soil of self-will and determination has left you more empty and lifeless than ever? Maybe God is inviting you right now to stop, to sit, to stay, to trust, to plant yourself deeply and wait and watch as he does in your life what he has been doing throughout human history. Maybe it's time for you to come to your Gardener God and offer back to him the life he promised could be yours. Will you do just about the only thing you can do . . . will you stay?

Single-minded Shepherd

Single-Minded Shepherd

I come from a strange flock. My extended family members (on my mother's side) are all from different parts of New Mexico. They can be divided into two camps. One half are ranchers—hardworking, weatherworn people who have made their living from land and livestock. They are the real deal. The other half have chosen to make their way on the backs of others. They are chiropractors. How this profession emerged from the plains of Clayton is still a mystery to me. Many of them own a practice or have gone in together to form a nice little network of family chiropractors. This makes for outrageous family reunions. Every three years we all get together and spend a week laughing, talking, eating, drinking, playing, dancing, and getting readjusted. Friday nights are reserved for the dance. All of us huddled into the meeting room of a YMCA camp with sounds of country music (the real kind) pouring out of the rustic windows. It's picture-perfect: children dancing with parents, the slimming number of patriarchs and matriarchs watching in divine amusement. As the dance winds down, the tables come out. Lines begin to form as

Uncle Lymon, his son Derrick, and Little Paul (who's actually 6'4") begin to un-work the damage wrought from the week's events. Norman Rockwell would have killed to have this kind of inspiration.

Several of my childhood summers were spent on the ranch with the other half of my mother's side. I was a fish well out of water. Growing up as a California kid, this world was as exciting as it was exhausting. These days were spent in the fields, on the farm, and riding around in a beat-up pickup driven my cousin Chad, who at ten years old had already mastered the nuisances of the old Ford. Then there are the 4-H memories that seem more like a dream than anything I actually experienced. I knew nothing of this world, but I appreciated it. I respected the 5:00 a.m. breakfasts, the hot summer days, and the afternoon dips in the hot metal troughs that doubled as both swimming pool and watering hole for the cattle. It is a world that is all but forgotten in the American experience. A world that lives and breathes and provides for so much of what goes unappreciated in our ever urbanizing American ascent.

However, this was a world utterly familiar to the huddled masses that hung on Jesus' every word. A world that had a purpose and place. A world that was fodder to the many stories Jesus told. Throughout his life and teaching Jesus dipped his brush into the brilliant colors of everyday life to paint masterpiece images of the reality of God. He referred to seeds and weeds, trees and fruit, land and landowners. But one of the most frequently referenced ways of life was that of sheep and shepherd.

The pages of the Bible are littered with the deep imagery afforded by the shepherd's way of life. It was David himself who was known as the Shepherd King. Psalm 23 stands as his divine testament to God, the Good Shepherd.

And it was shepherds who were there, watching their flocks by night as the angels appeared and made known the birth of Jesus. Jesus borrows from this image as he describes both God and himself as the Good Shepherd, who knows his flock and whose flock knows him and his voice (John 10:27). He paints Satan as the thief who comes to steal and kill and destroy the flock (John 10:10) and the Pharisees as hired hands who care nothing for the flock (John 10:12–13). While Jesus' sheep stories and allusions vary, there is one constant—you and I are always the sheep. (Unless of course you count one of the most important "sheep" references in the entire Bible—Jesus, the Lamb of God who came to take away the sins of the world. That one is pretty important. Okay, so other than that one, we're always the sheep!)

The analogies are endless and more than a little embarrassing. Sheep are notoriously stupid and stubborn creatures. They are prone to wander, oftentimes into danger, and sometimes to their own demise. They are helpless to defend themselves against attack. They require constant care and attention. Phillip Keller, in his masterpiece *A Shepherd Looks at Psalm 23*, points out that sheep require more care and attention than any other animal. On top of all that, they stink. I'm not sure if this is a truth God meant for us to grapple with, but the fact remains, them sheep is some stanky creatures!

In Luke 15 Jesus paints a picture of the shepherd heart that God has for his beloved sheep. Jesus tells the story of a shepherd who at the end of a long day of . . . sheeping . . . notices that one of his sheep is not present. As he corrals his flock of a hundred sheep into the safety of the pen, he notices that something is not right. Out of a hundred sheep, he can tell that one is missing. Clearly he is more than a macro manager who cannot see the sheep

Like Sheep without a Shearer . . .

I heard a story about a wild sheep in New Zealand named Shrek, who had roamed free for over six years after escaping from its shepherd when it was young. The sheep never once had its fleece trimmed, which meant by the time it was finally found and captured, its fleece alone weighed over sixty pounds! That's sixty pounds of wool, enough to make twenty men's suits (or sixty if they came from the Men's Wearhouse). Its captors didn't even recognize Shrek as a sheep. I believe the direct quote was that they thought he was some sort of "biblical creature" (not quite sure from what part in the Bible, maybe the Apocrypha). Upon deciding it was time to cut Shrek's fleece, they did what any self-respecting, animal-loving person would do: they made a TV special out of it. Tens of thousands of people tuned in to watch an animal be shorn on live TV (ah, the thrill of it all). When it was all said and done, Shrek was a completely different creature, some sixty pounds lighter and ready to face the world. Shrek's not sure what he'll do next.

There are book rights, movie deals, grass to eat. The sky is the limit. But for now he just reminisces on the hairstyle that took him six years to grow, and why anyone would give up thirty minutes of their life to watch it all get cut off.

www.news.bbc.co.uk/1/hi/world/asia-pacific/3665735.stm

through the flock. He knows each sheep. He has most likely known them their entire lives. The way he knows one is missing is not through a roll call or head count. He can sense the absence of its presence. And so he does what any good shepherd would do, he leaves the ninety-nine that are safe to go and hunt down the one that is lost.

[Christ] did ... promise enough joy and courage, enough love and confidence in God to enable those who went His way to do far more than survive. Because they would be in harmony with the very Life and Spirit of God, they would be able to defeat evil. They would be able to take the initiative and destroy evil with good.

J. B. Phillips

To fully understand this image of God, we have to remember what it is like to be helplessly lost. Whether you were hiding inside the clothing racks at Sears only to emerge to find that your mom was nowhere to be found, or whether it was somewhere within the mall proper, or whether you got lost in the shuffle of a large crowd, we all know what it's like.

I remember being lost once at Chuck E. Cheese's. This was back when the name Chuck E. Cheese's actually meant something; it was the premiere place for fine quality arcade entertainment and mediocre pizza. It used to be a big place, not today's strip mall shadow of its former self. Chuck E. Cheese's was huge, an endless maze of arcades, lip-synching costumed characters, and row upon row of skeeball pandemonium. Dining room after dining room filled with screaming kids and their parents.

It happened somewhere around Asteroids. I was lost in my game, too preoccupied to notice that my dad had left. At first I thought nothing of it. I assured myself that we would find each other sooner or later, but sooner was taking longer than I liked, and I began to panic. After about fifteen minutes, I began to think that the robotic hands clapping on the walls were not automated as I had assumed, but were actually the hands of all the other little children who had been lost here before me. In a moment of desperate brilliance, I went to the microphone where they call out the orders and asked them to page my dad. When they asked what his name was, I froze from my franticness, and all I could muster was "Dad." They asked me to be more specific, so I dove deep into the recesses of my elementary mind and tried to remember what it was that my mom had called him the other night . . . "chauvinist" . . . no . . . "no good" . . . no . . . STEVE! That's it: Steve! Within moments of the page, Steve, aka Dad, came meandering toward me, pizza in hand, utterly unaware of the drama I had endured. While my panic only lasted a few moments, it was enough of a scare to stay with me years later. It's a feeling you don't quickly forget.

It is that paralyzing, familiar sense of being lost that Jesus is evoking. The desperation that settles in and convinces you that all hope is lost, the fear that hijacks your better judgment, the shame of knowing that it was you who wandered off. For we all, like sheep, have wandered off, gotten lost, gone astray. It is into this reality that the Good Shepherd steps in.

At first glance, the image Jesus paints of a Good Shepherd may seem foreign to us, because it is. We have a very small framework to understand a Middle Eastern shepherd's reality from two thousand years ago. Even the parts of the world where sheep herding is still a vital part of the economy and ecology are still far off and unfamiliar. But the love that this Shepherd has for his sheep should ring true for anyone who has ever loved a pet. There is a beautiful neuroticism that is shared among animal lovers. We would do anything for our pets. They are not beasts, but friends, companions, members of the family. They bring joy and laughter. They appear in family Christmas pictures. They do very little for us, and yet we would do almost anything for them.

Recently while playing catch with our yellow Lab Molly, I saw just what I would do for an animal. We were in the middle of a rousing game of "throw the stick, fetch the stick" when Molly made a sound I had never heard before. Apparently the stick had stuck in the ground after my throw, and upon retrieval, Molly gouged her mouth underneath her tongue. She yelped and jumped back and then stood there dazed and confused. I called her over to inspect the damage and could see that she was bleeding. I immediately went into triage mode. I cleaned her up, gave her water to wash out the cut, and brought her inside. My wife and I noticed she was moving slowly and lethargically. We figured she was just scared and let her rest for a while inside. Hours later when we went to bed, Molly could barely make it up the stairs. We called to her and she just looked at us; it was as though she couldn't even hear us. Jeanne became worried and invited Molly up into our bed, an invitation she would normally not refuse. But instead of jumping up, she just laid there, almost catatonic. I told Jeanne not to worry about it and that we would take her to the vet in the morning, but my words were meaningless. Jeanne stayed up with Molly for hours, watching and comforting her. At around two in the morning, Molly began moaning and having what appeared to be small convulsions. That was all Jeanne needed. She ran downstairs, found the phonebook, and called the nearest twenty-four-hour animal hospital ... thirty minutes away!

We love our dog Molly ... maybe a little too much. As a symbol of our love, we took our family Christmas picture with her a few years back ... in our bathtub. We thought it would be funny, apparently we were just about the only ones.

Have a Merry Christmas
and a Happy New Year!

Love Jarrett, Jeannie,
and Molly

In case you're wondering, yes we have our swimsuits on, and no, we don't do this every week ... it's actually every other.

We swooped Molly up, put her in the car, and began our late-night trek. Those thirty minutes in the car felt like hours as my wife held our sixty-five-pound dog in her arms, comforting her through her own tears. It took ten minutes and two hundred dollars to find out what was wrong. Molly was in shock from the wound, but she would be fine. After a few shots for her and a few sedatives for us, we put her in the car and made our way back home. We arrived at 3:30 a.m. and Molly had regained just enough energy to jump into our bed and spend the few remaining hours of sleep in the comfort of her masters' care. By the next morning, she was back to her old self as if nothing had ever happened. But something had happened. Our love for a dog, a silly little animal, was fully revealed and realized. It became quite obvious to us at 3:30 in the morning that we would do just about anything for her.

If you've never owned a pet, or if you've only ever had tropical fish, then you have no idea about this kind of fanatical love people have for their pets. But if you have owned and loved a pet, you know exactly what Jesus is talking about. A good shepherd is one who, like in Jesus' story about God, drops everything to do anything their pet requires. The image becomes that much clearer. You get why the shepherd in Jesus' story would risk his own life for the safety and recovery of his sheep's. You understand the overflow of love and joy that fills the heart of the shepherd upon the discovery of one little wandering sheep. "And when he finds it, he joyfully puts it on his shoulders and goes home. Then he calls his friends and neighbors together and says, 'Rejoice with me; I have found my lost sheep'" (Luke 15:5–6).

"He joyfully puts it on his shoulders ..." What a poignantly perfect image of God for us to rest in. Not only can we be found by God, but we will be joyfully lifted up out of the mess that we got ourselves into, and placed on the safe and strong shoulders of a shepherd who loves us. There is no shame in this image. There is no need to give a good excuse for why we wandered so far. There is only joy and love and safety. There is only the devotion of a shepherd to his lost sheep. There is only the wonderful surprise of being found. What an image. What an opportunity. What a God, who would leave everything, who would risk everything, to come and find you right where you are.

It was in the midst of countless images of great loss that we saw a glimpse of the search and rescue heart of God. In the wake of Hurricane Katrina, one of the greatest natural disasters and political debacles America has ever seen, there were so many horrific images of devastation and isolation. Amidst the onslaught of twenty-four-hour cable news coverage, there was one image that stands out as we begin to more deeply reflect on God as a Good Shepherd. I wonder if you saw it.

It was the image of a man, who after almost a week of waiting to be rescued, refused to get aboard a bus that was finally ready to take him to safety. After all he had suffered, he refused to leave the spot on the side of the road that he had occupied. His reason? They wouldn't allow his dog on the bus with him. His safety was forcibly contingent upon his ability to abandon his dog. In the midst of this chaos, Nate Berkus (a regular correspondent for Oprah Winfrey, a man who had suffered his own personal loss in the tsunami that devastated Sri Lanka only months before ... and also someone my wife has a gigantic crush on) received news of this man. Nate personally committed in that moment to put the dog in his car and follow the man to wherever he was being taken. The man broke down and wept in Nate's arms over the relief of knowing his dog would be safe. This was not another self-aggrandizing camera hogging moment. This was one pet lover loving another. The next day, as promised, the man was reunited with his dog in the safety of a shelter over a hundred miles away.

It's a powerful story. The stuff Oprah episodes are made of. But more important, it's the stuff of which great stories are made. Jesus stories. Stories about Good Shepherds and Lost Sheep. Stories that don't make sense. Why would someone care so much for an animal? Why would someone be willing to sacrifice their own comfort and safety for the sake of a dog ... or a sheep ... or you and me? I don't know. All I know is that each of us knows in one way or another what it means to be lost. Whether it's in the middle of Chuck E. Cheese's or in the middle of Nebraska or in the middle of your sophomore year in college. Whether you're lost in your career or lost within a dead marriage, whatever it is, the point is you understand how it feels to be utterly lost and alone without any sense of home. We all do. The unique opportunity, however, is for us to be found. Wherever your wayward heart has led you, you can know what it is like to be found. Right now. There is God who has left everything to find you, right where you are. Will you let him take you home again? Will you let yourself be found?

For "you were like sheep going astray,"
but now you have returned to the Shepherd
and Overseer of your souls.

1 Peter 2:25

Tired-eyed Father

Tired-Eyed Father

There is a story that has been told for thousands of years. It has been told and retold countless times. In all its telling, it has become legendary. It's one you have probably heard before; in fact, it may be the most recognizable story in this book. But somehow, in all the hearing, we may have missed its power.

Over the years, the foundation of this story has shifted and given way from father to son. A prodigal son. First of all, no one even knows what "prodigal" means anymore (prä-di-gəl: rashly or wastefully extravagant). Second, it's not really a story about a rashly or wastefully extravagant son, but of a faithful and forgiving father. It's a story about a father who reveals the essence of Abba God.

In Luke 15 Jesus tells the story of a son who, after looking at his family's assets, decides it's time to cash in and move out. He demands that his father give him his share of his inheritance now. From the estimated value of the family home, to his college fund, to his share of his father's life insurance policy, to half of the net worth of the family business. He wanted it all, and he wanted it now.

So the father gave it to him. No protest, no argument; for no good reason, the father gives the son exactly what he asks for. And just like that, the son is gone.

He hit the road and traveled far away from his father, to a place where nobody knew his name or where his money came from. They couldn't care less, so long as it kept flowing. And flow it did! The son wasted no time in wasting all of his money. There were parties, there were women, there were weekends that existed only as a blur. But, as the story goes, within a few short months, all that the father had given to the son was gone, with nothing to show for it other than empty pockets of shame and regret. He was broke, empty, and alone. To make matters worse, a famine hit the land in which he was living. Now a starving stranger in a strange and starving land, he was desperate. He took work as a foreigner feeding the pigs that gorged themselves on the waste of society. In his desperate desolation, he began to look at the trash that he fed to the pigs and began to wonder what it might taste like. He was a world away from the familiar smells that escaped from his father's kitchen. He lived as long as he could on those memories until his soul was famished.

Under the unforgiving sun of that foreign land, he began to reason to himself that maybe if he went crawling back to his father, that maybe, by some slim chance, his father might hire him as a servant where at least he could eat at a table, with utensils, with his father's roof over his head. He began to go over the speech he would deliver to his father upon his arrival. He mulled over every word, trying to capture the shame and remorse he felt for all he had said and done. If all went well, maybe his father would take him back in as a servant, working the rest of his life to pay off the debt he had incurred. This was his plan.

Much has been written about Rembrandt's painting *The Return of the Prodigal*, the most formational of which is Henri Nouwen's *The Return of the Prodigal Son*. The entire book is a reflection on each of the characters in the painting below. Upon reflection on the love the father has for us, Nouwen writes, "Here the mystery of life is unveiled. I am loved so much that I am left free to leave home. The blessing is there from the beginning. I have left it and keep on leaving it. But the Father is always looking for me with outstretched arms to receive me back and whisper again in my ear: 'You are my Beloved, on you my favor rests.'"[1]

I will not attempt to add more to Nouwen's work. But I would like to offer you some time and space. So before you read another word of this book, stop. Be still. Reflect on the depth of God's love revealed to you through this story and this image.

1. Henri Nouwen, *The Return of the Prodigal Son* (New York: Doubleday, 1992).

So he set off for home. His feet slowly shuffling and struggling under the weight of all he had done. He crossed his father's property line at the point of exhaustion. At least, he reasoned, he would die on familiar soil. But before he could muster the strength for another step, he saw on the flickering line of the horizon, a figure. It grew in size and familiarity as it drew closer. It was his father, coming—no running—toward him. The son had never imagined what would happen next: the father wrapped his arms around this poor prodigal and wept aloud at the joy of his return. Fear and fatigue were met with love and grace. The father swept his son's frail body up in his arms once more and carried him back to the home he had abandoned. The son tried to spit his speech out, but the father didn't hear him, he was too busy shouting to the servants to bring clothes and food, and to prepare the welcome home party they had been planning since the day the son left. The son was welcomed back as though he never left. He was home. Not in the house of his youth, but in the arms of his father who lovingly and patiently watched and waited for his return.

This is the story Jesus gives us to illuminate the deep complexity of the father's love for us. This is the picture he paints. This is the invitation he gives. This is Abba. The Abba of Jesus. No amount of wandering or squandering can separate you from his love. He invites you to look long into his loving gaze. He invites you to bask in his deep delight over you, even in the midst of your darkest defeat. He invites you to accept the safety and security of his embrace. He longs to listen to you, even when you don't have the words to talk. He is your Abba, and according to Jesus, you are his beloved child.

Again and again Jesus spoke of Almighty God as his Abba. A word very familiar to Jesus, but less familiar to us.

ABBA, the band, not to be confused with Abba, the deity

It's a name that has been spoken for thousands of years. A name that Jesus knew intimately. A name at the center of this story.

There has been much study and research done on this colloquial little word. Many have devoted their entire lives to understanding it and living out of it. This study and work however is not to be confused with the findings of a small group of Swedish "theologians" in the late half of the twentieth century. And before we go any further into understanding Abba, we have to set one thing straight. The Abba that Jesus spoke of had nothing to do with the satin and polyester-clad seventies Swedish super group known as ABBA. As important as they are, they have little to nothing to do with this image of Jesus that Jesus taught us about. I know you know this, but I feel it necessary to mention it now so you won't giggle as you thumb through the pages of this chapter. So why don't you just get it out now.

The significance of Jesus' use of the name "Abba" is that, for the first-century Jew, it would have been completely irreverent and utterly unthinkable to call God by such a familiar word. Jesus lived among a people who had such devout reverence for God that they wouldn't even say his name—Yahweh. The utterance of his name led to a most certain, and probably uncomfortable, death. In Jesus' day, there was an established system of worship involving complex hierarchal layers of rabbis, Pharisees, priests, and high priests. The temple itself was designed to keep God in the Holiest of Holy places, separated from the common everyday people. There was an incredible level of reverence and respect for God. And then came Jesus.

Jesus came into this context not only claiming to be the Son of God (which is enough in itself to get one killed) but he called God his Abba, his Daddy. This powerful prophet, this mighty miracle worker, this respected rabbi, this thirty-year-old man calling God his Abba. This was not the best way to earn respect from the masses. If only Jesus had had an image consultant, he might not have said things like, "Hear O Israel, my Daddy is an awesome God. And my Daddy and I are one!" (see Mark 12:29).

But Jesus' use of "Abba" was never meant to be metaphorical or allegorical like some sort of object lesson for future generations. No, this is who God was (is) to Jesus. This is what Jesus called him as a child, this is what he called him alone in his times of prayer, and this is what he called him in front of the crowds he taught and walked with. God is the Abba of Jesus. A name he knew and a voice he recognized his entire life. We hear from the Abba of Jesus first at his baptism.

As soon as Jesus was baptized, he went up out of the water. At that moment heaven was opened, and he saw the Spirit of God descending like a dove and alighting on him. And a voice from heaven said, "This is my Son, whom I love; with him I am well pleased."

Matthew 3:16–17

It's important to see when this Abba experience is happening. It's at Jesus' baptism, at the very beginning of his public ministry. Before Jesus *did* anything. Before he performed any miracles. Before he gave any great sermons. Before he called any disciples. He heard and recognized that he was loved by his Abba. It was the voice of his Abba that would carry him through his forty days in the wilderness, where he was tempted to listen to and claim his identity in anything other than his Abba. But his way was set. He knew who he belonged to. The life of Jesus was radically defined by the love of his Abba long before he ever did a thing.

But much has been lost in translation. We are far from being able to recognize and rest in the voice of Abba amidst the noise of our lives. And we have a hard time believing that we are loved long before we even lift a finger. But that is precisely what Jesus is revealing about the Father and exactly what he's inviting you and I into—to be able to hear and know the voice of our Abba God who loves us, and in the absence of fear and formality, to be able to speak back to him.

If once we accept it as true that the whole Power behind this astonishing Universe is that kind of character that Christ could only describe as "Father," the whole of life is transfigured.

J. B. Phillips

If John 3:16 is the most recognized verse from the Bible, then the Lord's Prayer is the most recognized prayer. It has been prayed from a plethora of pulpits, memorized in countless confirmation classes, and uttered on desperate deathbeds. You might know it as the "Our Father" (still one of the best names for a prayer, right next to the "Oh God, please don't let him write me a ticket" and the "Oh God, I think I'm going to puke"). This prayer is so familiar that we almost overlook it. In fact, I'll bet all the money in the offering plate that you know it, or at least know the first couple lines. Found in chapter 6 of Matthew, it goes something like: "Our Father, who art in heaven, hallowed be thy name. Thy kingdom come, thy will be done, on earth as it is in heaven. Give us this day our blah, blah, blah. And forgive us our blah, as we blah, blah, blah ..." Does that ring a bell?

This beautiful prayer has become drab and dull from centuries of memorization and repetition. Its words now blur together into a singsong monotony devoid of the power and intimacy with which it was first uttered. When Jesus was asked by his disciples how they should pray, he didn't just give them words to memorize or a form to follow; rather, he gave them a deep and personal way to experience Abba. The prayer actually starts with a cry to Abba. Jesus said, "Pray like this, 'Our Abba in heaven, honored be your name.' "

How the temperature changes when we pray to our Abba and not some distant and deaf deity who has all but forgotten the words himself. Suddenly this prayer comes into focus. The language is critical. Jesus chose every word with a reason. And the first word we are to utter in prayer is "Abba." When we start with "Abba," every word that follows is suddenly different.

So often, I'll catch myself in the middle of a prayer saying words that I would never use with a friend or with my Daddy. Seriously, when was the last time you heard anyone use the word "hallowed"? "Did you see that new Leonardo DiCaprio film? It was so hallowed. I would love to crown that director with many crowns."

I'm not totally convinced that I even understand all the words I use when I pray. Maybe this is why so many people are afraid to pray in front of others. I know a woman in her fifties who still to this day won't pray out loud. She's actually a leader in her church, which is how I met her. Every time a group of us would gather to pray, she remained silent. Eventually, out of frustration and intrigue, I asked her to pray for me (not the most honest of motives, but I just had to know). She told me she would be glad to later on that night. When I asked her why she wouldn't just pray for me right there, she told me she just didn't feel comfortable praying out loud. I asked her how a woman who has walked so long with God and been so active in church would still feel uncomfortable about praying out loud. She told me that it wasn't that she felt uncomfortable, but rather insecure. She was afraid she would say something simple, something stupid, something that would reveal the truth about herself—that she actually didn't know all of the insider words and phrases that people throw around when they pray. She felt better when she could just think her prayers to God quietly.

I felt so sorry for her, so worried about getting it wrong or saying something that revealed her "level" of spirituality. How much further from the point can you get than that? The point of prayer is not to be poetic or brilliant or spiritual or to get the most people to say "hmmm," or to impress God with your vernacular acrobatics. The point is Abba! He is the point of our prayer. If we are praying to our Daddy whom we trust, then we have nothing to hide or change, no reason to impress him or anybody else who might be listening. Before your language can ever be beautiful, it has to be personal. Before any sense of intricacy, must come intimacy. If your prayer starts with Abba, it changes every word that follows.

We see this personal intimacy in living color, when no one is around in the garden of Gethsemane, just hours before Jesus is arrested and ultimately crucified. In Jesus' greatest hour of need, who does he pray to?

> *"Abba, Father," he said, "everything is possible*
> *for you. Take this cup from me. Yet not*
> *what I will, but what you will."*

Mark 14:36

It is to Abba that Jesus makes his garden plea. Abba ... Daddy ... please. And yet because of his trust in his Abba, he chose to obey his Abba's way, and not his own.

When your prayer starts with Abba, it begins to change everything about you.

Jesus has invited us into the most intimate relationship with his Abba. A life of hearing and recognizing the voice of Abba that tells you how much he loves you. "As the Father has loved me, so have I loved you. Now remain in my love" (John 15:9). A life of living in and out of the love of Abba. A life of claiming your very identity in him and a life of speaking to him. No longer living in fear, like someone who doesn't know him. In the book of Romans, it says, "God's Spirit touches our spirits and confirms who we really are. We know who he is, and we know who we are: Father and children" (8:16 MSG).

Imagine again the intimacy of the embrace between wayward child and faithful father from Jesus' story. Go back to Rembrandt's picture if you need to. Place yourself in that moment, in that embrace. There in the tear-soaked chest of your Abba God. What is it in that moment that you need to hear from your Abba? Take a moment to reflect on these words. Think of some of your own, or if you like to keep a journal, write them down.

You are my beloved child. I loved you before you could ever attempt to do anything to impress me or earn my love.

You are forgiven. I know what you've done, I know how far you've gone. But take heart, there's nothing you can do that can separate my love from you.

You are my beautiful creation. I am so proud of you.

Let these words soak in. Meditate on them. Memorize them. Keep them on your desk at work or in your medicine cabinet at home. It would serve us well to daily break through the noise and distraction of our lives and sit in the silent truth of God's deep love for us. And not just sit, but also speak. Go back to the moment of that intimate embrace. You are there. Your Abba is there. If you truly believed you were loved and safe, what would you want to say to your Abba God?

> *I love you. I love you more than myself, my life, my family, my career, my stuff, my religion, my*
>
> _____.
>
> *I'm sorry. Forgive me.*
> *You are my God, my Father, my life, my home.*
> *Thank you.*

I have found this simple little exercise to be one of the greatest things I can do to allow the reality of Abba to be fully formed in my life. To stop pretending, to stop running, to come home and know the God of the universe as my Abba. This has proven to be the single most difficult and life-changing reality of God for me to embrace. My heart longed for it to be true, but my head told me it was impossible. That there had to be more. And yet I've found that this is it. This, in so many ways, is where my journey has led me—into the arms of my Abba. It is the safest and scariest place I have ever been. It is a place I had to choose to go, a place I needed help getting to, and a place I never want to leave. It is a place I hope you find as well.

NOW HIRING!

Equal Opportunity Employer

*N*o matter what anyone may say, my résumé totally rocks. No employer in the world can deny the drive and determination that has brought me to where I am today. My career began when I was fourteen. It was the start of my freshman year, and my mom informed me that I would be buying my own clothes from that moment on. Most fourteen-year-olds would crumble at this announcement. Not me. I went out and got me a J-O-B. It all started with D & D Bicycles. With a name like "D & D Bicycles" I secretly hoped to be greeted by Dungeon Masters with level 4 magic abilities holding eight-sided dice. No such luck. D & D was a bicycle painting company located at the end of an inconspicuous row of industrial warehouses in the middle of San Leandro, California. I worked with Rick and Rick, two twentysomethings who couldn't have been any more opposite if they tried. Rick #1 was the skinny, quiet type who kept mostly to himself (and probably played D & D). Rick #2 was five times the man of

Rick #1. Clocking in at six feet tall and four feet wide, Rick #2 was loud, obnoxious, and covered in tattoos (before it was cool). He was the front man of a hardcore band with a name so "hardcore," it could never get published in this book. Within fifteen minutes of showing up, I was put on the sandblasting machine, an archaic beast of a machine that I'm sure was used in the atomic bomb labs of World War II. I wasn't paid all that much, but then again, I didn't do that much. After a couple months of blasting bikes, I convinced myself that I was overqualified and was off to a bigger and better career.

After a tearful good-bye from Ricks 1 and 2, I made my way to Blockbuster Video. After being assured that I wouldn't have to work with sand in any capacity, I took a job as a C.S.R. (customer service representative). I even had a blue and yellow name badge to remind me who I was. I was official. I spent an entire year making people's Thursday night action-adventure dreams a reality. But as much as I loved my khaki-pant and faux-denim-shirt life, I began to feel that undeniable call of the road. I left Block-buster to pursue a career in the domestic foods export industry.

My job as the delivery boy at Blackhawk Pizzeria was all I hoped it would be. Fast-paced and free-spirited, with all the tips I could stuff into my leather pouch. We called ourselves "drivers" and catered to some of the wealthiest sports stars and self-made millionaires of San Francisco's East Bay. I finally had a job that paid more than $4.25 an hour and left me with the inescapable aroma of garlic on everything I owned. I worked hard and was paid well (mostly under the table of course).

Eventually, I would land a job as a part-time junior high drama teacher while in college. During that time I also took work as the youth ministry intern at my church, which basically meant I was the one who had to wait after the all night lock-in until the last of the parents showed to pick up their kids. It also meant that I was the permanent designated driver of the church's 1973 avocado-green twelve-passenger van. It was an unbreakable bulk of army grade metal that had given up on the concept of brakes sometime back in the early eighties.

None of these jobs paid very much, but they didn't need to. These jobs, as lame as some of them may seem to you, were forging in me what my artist friends feared most: a work ethic. And while daydreams of a utopian society where socialism actually works may have passed through my mind during my mandatory fifteen-minute breaks behind the mall, I knew the truth: those who work hard and do a good job will be paid accordingly (even if it is $4.25 an hour).

Since the age of fourteen I've always had a job. I've always had to work. And I've always had a paycheck (and believe me, I am grateful). Over the years of building such a rockin' résumé, I've come to appreciate that age-old dance of employer-employee. There is a beautiful consistency and simplicity to it all. Do your job and you will be paid. Do your job well and you may even get a raise. Who knows, they may even raise your weekly video rental allowance from two videos to four, so long as they're not new releases. It is this beautiful consistency and simplicity that lies as one of the bedrocks to the human experience. It's as old as antiquity. A balance present in every great society. A principle that is understood in every culture. A balance that would be turned completely upside down through the teaching of Jesus on the (un)fair heart of God.

In Matthew 20 Jesus tells the story of a landowner who needed some help. So he did what most short-staffed landowners would do: he went down to the center of town to find some day laborers. This was a completely common practice in the day of Jesus and still is almost anywhere you go. Perhaps you've seen it early in the morning; whether it's in the industrial part of town or out in the fields, they are there. Men who desperately desire to be chosen in a labor lottery that plays out every single day all over the world. It doesn't matter what the work, so long as there's a fair wage at the end. With the word "fair" becoming increasingly relative as the cupboard grows more bare. This is the reality of the day laborer, one all too familiar to the hardworking people of Jesus' day. His story is already off to a great start, and his listeners are tracking.

Christ had no bias and no theory: He came to give us the facts, and they are quite plainly, that this "power-to-love" which He recommended should be expended on God and other people, has been turned in on itself.

J. B. Phillips

Jesus goes on to tell how this landowner finds his first batch of workers in the slow, gray hours of the early morning. They agree upon a denarius for a day's work—a fair amount for that time—and he sends them off to work in his vineyard. At about 9:00 a.m. the landowner goes back to the center of town and sees a large, humbled huddle of men who had not been chosen that day. It's 9:00 a.m. All the day laborers had already been chosen. They were picked through and left standing, waiting, hoping that maybe a landowner somewhere got a late start to his day. Or, in the case of their blessed fortune, a landowner needed more help. More men were chosen, and after being told they would be paid "fairly" (you're not really in

Let's face it, working for minimum wage can be a drag. But as bad as it can get, there's always that little voice in your head that tries to convince you to be thankful you have a job, and that you live in a country that takes care of its minimum wagers. It's a sweet thought, but I bet that little voice in your head never told you what they make in Switzerland! Check out the monthly minimum wage earnings from around the world, and start packing your bags.

Monthly Minimum Wage Incomes from around the World (As of July 11, 2005)

Country	Monthly Minimum Wage (In U.S. Dollars)
Switzerland	$2,330 (Almost three times what the average American makes! The grass truly is greener on the other side of the Atlantic.)
The Netherlands	$1,507

France	$1,468 (Hate on France all you want, but the dude flipping your Royale with Cheese is still making almost twice as much as you.)
Canada	$1444
United States	$824 (Once again, the United States is holding a commanding position ... right in the middle.)
Mexico	$664
Brazil	$128 (Sure it's seven times less than what the average American makes, but come on, it's Brazil!)
Bulgaria	$95 (Sure it's eight times less than what the average American makes, but come on, it's Bulgaria!)[1]

---

1. *http://en.wikipedia.org/wiki/Minimum_wage*

any sort of position to negotiate at 9:00 a.m.) they went off to work. But this landowner's day was far from over. He went back over at the lunch hour and again at 3:00 p.m. and picked more laborers, telling each of them they would be paid fairly. Finally at 5:00 p.m., just an hour before the end of the workday, the landowner went out once more and hired the last remaining few. There is most likely a good reason why these men went eleven hours without being chosen. The laws of labor can be cruel, but they are consistent. It is safe to assume these men had very little to offer the average employer. It's even safer to assume that the 6:00 p.m. walk from the center of town to the shantytown shacks they called home was one of the most defeating and demeaning walks they had to endure. A daily ritual that would be broken that day. Here, just one hour before closing time, they are hired. The landowner assures them they will be paid fairly, which means very little to them. To be paid at all was enough.

Before the last group of laborers had even broken a sweat, all of the employees are called together and given their "fair" wage. The landowner decides that those he picked up last would be paid first. Imagine their shock when they each received a full denarius. A day's wage for one hour of work! It was the best deal they ever received and the most money they had ever held in their humble hands. By the time this happened, the news was way to the back of the line, to those who had been hired twelve hours earlier, and their minds began to race. They reasoned, "If those men were paid a denarius for one hour's worth of work, surely we will be paid twelve denarii. Two weeks' wages for one day's work! Someone get this guy's business card." So imagine their shock and awe when they received exactly what the landowner had promised them in that early morning agreement—one denarius. A day's wage. It was fair. It was what they had agreed upon. But it was all wrong. They argued. They protested. They threatened to form a union and strike. Unfortunately for them, no one had ever heard of a union before.

The landowner simply responded:

> *"Friend, I am not being unfair to you.
> Didn't you agree to work for a denarius? Take your pay
> and go. I want to give the one who was hired last
> the same as I gave you. Don't I have the right to do
> what I want with my own money? Or are you
> envious because I am generous?"*

Matthew 20:13–15

With that, Jesus concluded his story, and in so doing, pulled the curtain back that much further on the wonderfully complicated heart of God. It is a simple story that was anything but simple to those who heard it for the first time. Anyone with any sense of justice or fairness would be appalled. What about workers' rights? What about fair wage laws? Why should someone who does less be treated equally? Jesus' story about the open heart of God was not some philosophical proposition that is best mulled over with a cup of coffee in hand. It was a direct response to the clouded hearts of some of his closest friends.

In Matthew 19, just moments before Jesus told this story, two very important things happened. First, Jesus was approached by someone we have come to call the Rich Young Ruler. His story is a sad sort of legend. He came to Jesus asking what he needed to do to "get" eternal life. This was apparently a man who had it all—wealth, authority, a good reputation, a good religious backbone—all this wrapped in the handsome package of youth. He had already made quite a life for himself. All that was left on his ambitious to-do list was to acquire eternal life. Jesus, knowing his heart, told him the best thing for him to do would be to free himself from the life he had worked so hard to build, to sell all his possessions and give the money to people who hadn't worked as hard as he. The Rich Young Ruler cannot find the faith to open the door to the storehouse of the thing he calls life and sadly walks away. As if he had been sleeping through the last five minutes, Peter blurts out to Jesus, "We have left everything to follow you! What then will there be for us?" (Matthew 19:27).

Jesus assures him that all who have given in to God's economy will be rightly rewarded in heaven, but there will be many who think they have earned eternal life who will find themselves in the back of the line.

This isn't the first story like this that Jesus told, and it wouldn't be the last. The upside-down redefinition of "fairness" was utterly important to his life and teachings. It is utterly important to the heart of God. It stands in direct contrast to what really matters most to us. We accept and ascribe to the concept of grace insomuch as it affects our own lives. It's in the acceptance of grace and extending it to others that we get it all wrong. We, the rich young rulers of the world, the ones who were picked up at 6:00 a.m. and have worked hard our whole lives, want to be rightly rewarded. There's a reason we have made it to where we are today. There's a reason why others haven't. Either they haven't worked hard enough or they don't want it badly enough. It doesn't really matter; all that matters is that things are fair. That we are acknowledged and properly rewarded for who we are and for what we have done. If someone wants to sneak in at the last minute, that's fine, but they're gonna have to wait their turn. They're gonna have to wait in the back. It's nothing personal; it's just the way it is. It's just fair.

The problem with our one-sided, earn-your-way-to-the-table-of-grace is that it has nothing to do with the heart of God. God is not fair. Not in the way we have come to define the term. He doesn't play by our rules, or set his scale to our measurements. God turns fair upside down. He sits the unemployed next to the self-made. He sits the drug addict next to the self-righteous. He sits the sick next to the healthy. The AIDS orphan next to the soccer mom. And he sits the one who showed up in the final moments of the workday next to the sweat-stained worker whose hands are so work-worn he can barely grab his own fork. In God's economy, all are rewarded by the disproportionate quotient of grace. No one is treated fairly or unfairly. Rather, all are rewarded with the gift of grace, the value of which is only fully appreciated by someone who understands who they really are and what they really deserve.

So afraid are we that we will not get what was promised us in the beginning, that we protest, complain, jockey for position, and suppress anyone who might get a piece of what is rightfully ours. With our résumés shoved firmly in the face of God, we make brilliant and compelling cases for why we deserve more grace than those poor souls in the back of the line. All the while forgetting that it was you and I who once stood at the back of the very line we have created.

This image of a God who will take anyone at any time is one that is easy to agree to on paper, but utterly challenging to accept in the everyday reality in which we live. Yet this is who God is. It is because of this God that Jesus had no issues partying with Matthew and his notoriously sinful friends. Because of this God, Jesus could embrace a woman who had sold her life away by the hour to whatever man would pay. Because of this God, Jesus could look to his left, to a murderous thief in the final few moments of his human existence, and cough out an invitation to paradise. It is why he could look down to those who had hung him on a cross to die and offer the forgiveness they weren't even asking for. It is because of this God that you and I, here in the place that this life has brought us, have a chance to join in on what God is doing, and has been doing for thousands of years. That's the crazy, unfair heart of God—it's never too late. Not for me. Not for you. Not for your brother, sister, husband, wife, mother, father, or anybody. This is the equal opportunity heart of God. One that never stops beating for those not yet in, not yet "fixed," not yet perfect, not yet even aware.

The End?

T'll never forget sitting in a dark movie theater with my dad and my best friend, Shadd. It was that week in between Christmas and New Year's. That magical time when all that is required of you is to eat, sleep in late, and play. The kind of week when it's okay to wear your pajamas until noon. We couldn't have been more than nine years old. And there we were, watching the cinematic masterpiece *Flash Gordon*. To the best of my knowledge we weren't wearing our pajamas. While much of that movie is forgettable, I was utterly mesmerized by the very last scene. All had ended well. The evil emperor, Ming the Merciless, was destroyed, his ring of power lay on the ground next to his ashes. But then, after all the resolve, I heard his evil laugh echoing in the background, and the words "The End" came on screen. Not too shocking ... until a question mark suddenly appeared: "The End?" The End? Was it? Was there more? Was Ming still alive? Was there another cheesy Queen song to be played? How could they do this to me? At nine years old I did not have the emotional capacity to deal with that sort of unresolve.

We waited through what seemed like an eternity of credits hoping for a clue. No clue came. Shadd and I then waited years for a *Flash Gordon* sequel. We would bring it up from time to time, but alas, there was no sequel made. After recently watching the movie again, I resolved that I should probably be grateful they never made a sequel. One *Flash Gordon* movie is all this world can handle.

Even though the movie was a flop, the idea was brilliant. The producers planted a seed in my nine-year-old mind that lives there to this day: There's more to come. The story doesn't have to end. Maybe, just maybe, it's not really the end, but a whole other beginning!

That's the whole idea of this book—that this isn't just the end of another book about God. Instead, I hope this book is the beginning of a whole new way of seeing and experiencing God. May this not be the end, but the beginning of honest questions and interesting conversations. May this be the beginning of a new journey for you into who God really is and who you really are in light of that reality.

Questions for Conversation

Introduction

1. What's your picture of God? Describe God in up to a dozen words or phrases:

   God is ...

   God is like a ...

2. What sources have contributed to your version of God?

Cop around the Corner

1. What do you do when you get caught doing something you shouldn't? What do you do to avoid getting caught, or when you fear you might get caught?

2. What people or experiences have encouraged you to see God as an authority figure waiting to nail you? (Or, what experiences have encouraged you *not* to see God like this?)

3. To what extent is your life built around playing by the rules? What does this look like in your life?

4. What are your top six "Thou shalt nots" (page 27)? No matter how ridiculous they might seem, take a few moments to honestly reflect on the unwritten, unspoken commandments you grew up with or learned along the way. How have they shaped who you are and how you interact with God?

5. Complete this sentence: If God catches me breaking one of these rules, he _____.

Sweet Old Man

1. What do you think about "old"? What positive or nega-tive associations do you have with oldness?

2. To what degree do you appreciate oldness in church? To what degree do you prefer newness? Why is that?

3. What aspects of the Bible seem old to you in a nega-tive way? What aspects seem current?

4. Is it appealing for you to think of God as safely retired somewhere else, but available by phone if you need him? Why or why not?

5. Are there parts of your world that you feel God is too old-fashioned to understand? If so, what are they?

6. What does it mean to say "time is a construct that God is not bound to"? If this is true, how does it affect the way you view and relate to God?

7. Imagine God as "active, dynamic, and on the move." What might he be doing?

8. What might a timeless God want to say of the temporal and urgent issues of your life?

Cosmic Slot Machine

1. Think of some of the wins or blessings in your life. How have they affected the way you think of and deal with God?

2. Think of some of the losses in your life. How have they affected the way you think of and deal with God?

3. Are there any losses — your own or someone else's — that make you doubt either God's goodness or his involvement in the world? If so, what are they?

4. Do you tend to be a risk taker, or do you tend to play it safe? How does that play out in your relationship with God?

5. Look at the three conclusions listed on page 47. Which, if any, do you find convincing? If none of them, what do you believe instead?

6. How strongly do you believe or disbelieve that, in the end, you'll win? How do your actions reflect what you believe?

7. What would it look like for you to bet it all on God?

Talent Show Judge

1. Do you feel pressure to do more and be more? If so, what's the "more" you feel you need to do?

2. Where do you think the pressure comes from? (Church leaders? Parents? Friends? God? Yourself?)

3. Complete this sentence: If I don't do enough for God _____.

4. Does God delight in you? What makes you say that?

5. Do you delight in God? What makes you say that?

6. Given that there's always more to be done at church, what do you think is enough for you?

7. Given that you can always do more in your personal life with God, what is enough for you right now?

8. How can you tell the difference between resting in "enough" and being spiritually lazy?

All-You-Can-Eat Buffet

1. Has the God of nothingness ever appealed to you? If so, how? If not, why not?

2. Does the buffet God—take what you like and leave the rest—appeal to you? If so, what parts do you like? If not, why not?

3. Are there aspects of the Christian God that you'd prefer not to swallow? What are they?

4. Why might it be important to swallow those anyway?

5. Why does faith have to call something out of you in order to give you something that matters?

Your Parents ... Supersized

1. Do the exercise on page 84: Write down a significant shaping event or experience with your parents, good or bad. What has that event or experience led you to assume to be true of God?

2. Where do you see that assumption about God played out in your choices as a teen or as an adult?

3. What did you learn from your parents about God's ability and willingness to give you these things:

   affection

   acceptance

   strength

   tenderness

   authority

   stability

4. How have some recent choices from your life reflected these assumptions about God?

5. Describe the kind of parent each of your parents is/was. How are these descriptions like or unlike the way you see God?

6. What do you feel when you think about your parents and your choices in this way? (Blame? Grief? Gratitude? Loneliness?)

Show and Tell

1. Has Jesus wrecked your life in any ways? If so, how? If not, how do you respond to the idea of Jesus wrecking your life?

Late-Night Neighbor

1. How bold or reluctant are you in asking God for what you need and want? Why is that?

2. What past disappointments, if any, have affected the way you pray?

3. What do you really, really want from God?

4. What do you really truly need?

5. If God knows what we need, why does he want us to ask?

6. What are we to conclude about God if we ask passionately for something and it doesn't happen?

7. How do you think a person learns to expect good things from God? (For instance, do you try really hard to work up the psychological state of belief? Do you go to rousing prayer meetings with other people who pray boldly? Do you make a list and start asking for things, and let the feeling of expectation come when it comes?)

Lord of the Boardroom

1. Why would anybody not want God to be their king?

2. What valuable resources has God given you to invest?

3. Are you more like the guys who risked it all, or like the guy who was afraid to fail? Why is that?

4. Complete this sentence: If I fail, God _____.

5. Make your own list of ways God has been generous to you.

6. Why do you suppose we often aren't very impressed with God's generosity? Why do we see his justice (perhaps even distorted as his demanding expectations) so much more clearly?

7. How do you want to respond to God's generosity?

Green-Thumbed Gardener

1. What does the story of the gardener tell you about God?

2. What does it tell you about what it means to be human?

3. What does it mean to say that God the gardener has dirty fingernails? How do you respond to that?

4. "Before you go, you stay." What does staying involve, on a practical level?

5. Why is "staying" hard?

6. Why are we often intent on taking care of ourselves, instead of trusting God to care for us? What are some ways you do this?

7. "You have something of worth and wonder to give to this world." How believable or unbelievable is this to you? Is it promise or pressure? Why?

Single-Minded Shepherd

1. Have you ever been lost? When? What did you feel at the time? (Desperation, fear, shame ...)

2. What picture of God do you get from the story of the lost sheep? How would you describe this God?

3. How easy is it for you to identify with the need to be rescued? Why?

4. Why might a person not let herself or himself be found?

5. Some of us are lost in less-than-obvious ways: lost in pride or the compulsion to get ahead or the fear of what other people think of us. Are you lost in anything you're willing to admit to—even just to yourself or to one other person?

6. What goes through your mind when you think of God's willingness to do whatever it takes for you? Some options:

    I'm thrilled and grateful.

    I have trouble believing it because _____.

    I believe it, but I sort of take it for granted.

    It's kind of humiliating to be seen as a sheep or a pet.

7. Take a moment to picture yourself as a small child, lost until a loving adult finds you and wraps you in his or her strong, safe arms. What positive or negative emotions does this flight of imagination produce?

Tired-Eyed Father

1. Where do you see the father's love in Rembrandt's painting, *The Return of the Prodigal*?

2. Think about God saying to you, without your doing anything, "You are my Beloved, on you my favor rests." What goes on inside you as you take that in?

3. We leave the place of blessing, Abba's arms, and we keep on leaving it. Why do you leave?

4. As often as you leave, he takes you back. How do you deal with that?

5. What are your insecurities about prayer, if any?

6. What do you long to hear from your Abba?

7. What keeps you from hearing those words? What helps you hear them?

Equal Opportunity Employer

1. What has your spiritual journey looked like?

    One of the workers hired at 6:00 a.m. who has been working all day?

    One of those hired at 9:00?

    Hired at 12:00?

    Hired at 3:00?

    Hired so recently you've hardly done any work at all?

2. Do you generally feel that you're being treated as you deserve, better than you deserve, or worse than you deserve? How so?

3. Do you ever envy those whom God appears to be blessing more than they deserve, or at the very least, more than you? If so, whom do you envy?

4. Why do you suppose God rewards those who come to him at the last minute the same as those who work hard for him all their lives?

5. Does this mean it's not worth our while to put effort into serving God in this life? Why or why not?

6. To whom would God like you to join with him in extending his undeserved grace?

The End?

1. What will you take away from your time in this book?

The Person Formerly Known as You

Jarrett Stevens, author of
The Deity Formerly
Known as God

"The glory of God is a human being fully alive."

Irenaeus

Something happened throughout the course of human history. Something that was never intended to happen. We lost our "selves." We lost our God-given idea of identity. From the very creation of the world, God intended human beings to exist as living reflections of himself. But then sin brought a separation, not only between human beings and God, but between human beings and themselves, their true selves.

In a follow-up to *The Deity Formerly Known as God*, Jarrett Stevens attempts to recapture the truth that we are each uniquely created by God with an identity he intended us to live out. Once again presenting the reader with destructive images that we've created for ourselves, and then countering those with constructive images that God uses throughout Scripture to describe us, Stevens wants to help readers identify and release the false view they have of themselves and begin to embrace their true identity, the person God created them to be.

Softcover: 0-310-27115-0

ZONDERVAN®

GRAND RAPIDS, MICHIGAN 49530 USA

WWW.ZONDERVAN.COM

WILLOW
Willow Creek Association

Willow Creek Association
Vision, Training, Resources for Prevailing Churches

This resource was created to serve you and to help you build a local church that prevails. It is just one of many ministry tools that are part of the Willow Creek Resources® line, published by the Willow Creek Association together with Zondervan.

The Willow Creek Association (WCA) was created in 1992 to serve a rapidly growing number of churches from across the denominational spectrum that are committed to helping unchurched people become fully devoted followers of Christ. Membership in the WCA now numbers over 10,500 Member Churches worldwide from more than ninety denominations.

The Willow Creek Association links like-minded Christian leaders with each other and with strategic vision, training, and resources in order to help them build prevailing churches designed to reach their redemptive potential. Here are some of the ways the WCA does that.

- **A2: Building Prevailing Acts 2 Churches—Today**—an annual two-and-a-half day event, held at Willow Creek Community Church in South Barrington, Illinois, to explore strategies for building churches that reach out to seekers and build believers, and to discover new innovations and breakthroughs from Acts 2 churches around the country.

- **The Leadership Summit**—a once a year, two-and-a-half-day conference to envision and equip Christians with leadership gifts and responsibilities. Presented live at Willow Creek as well as via satellite broadcast to over one hundred locations across North America, this event is designed to increase the leadership effectiveness of pastors, ministry staff, volunteer church leaders, and Christians in the marketplace.

- **Ministry-Specific Conferences** — throughout each year the WCA hosts a variety of conferences and training events — both at Willow Creek's main campus and offsite, across the U.S., and around the world — targeting church leaders and volunteers in ministry-specific areas such as: evangelism, small groups, preaching and teaching, the arts, children, students, women, volunteers, stewardship, raising up resources, etc.

- **Willow Creek Resources®** — provides churches with trusted and field-tested ministry resources in such areas as leadership, evangelism, spiritual formation, spiritual gifts, small groups, stewardship, student ministry, children's ministry, the use of the arts — drama, media, contemporary music — and more.

- **WCA Member Benefits** — includes substantial discounts to WCA training events, a 20 percent discount on all Willow Creek Resources®, *Defining Moments* monthly audio journal for leaders, quarterly *Willow* magazine, access to a Members-Only section on WillowNet, monthly communications, and more. Member Churches also receive special discounts and premier services through WCA's growing number of ministry partners — Select Service Providers — and save an average of $500 annually depending on the level of engagement.

For specific information about WCA conferences, resources, membership, and other ministry services contact:

Willow Creek Association
P.O. Box 3188
Barrington, IL 60011-3188
Phone: 847-570-9812
Fax: 847-765-5046
www.willowcreek.com

We want to hear from you. Please send your comments about this
book to us in care of zreview@zondervan.com. Thank you.

GRAND RAPIDS, MICHIGAN 49530 USA

ZONDERVAN.COM/
AUTHOR**TRACKER**